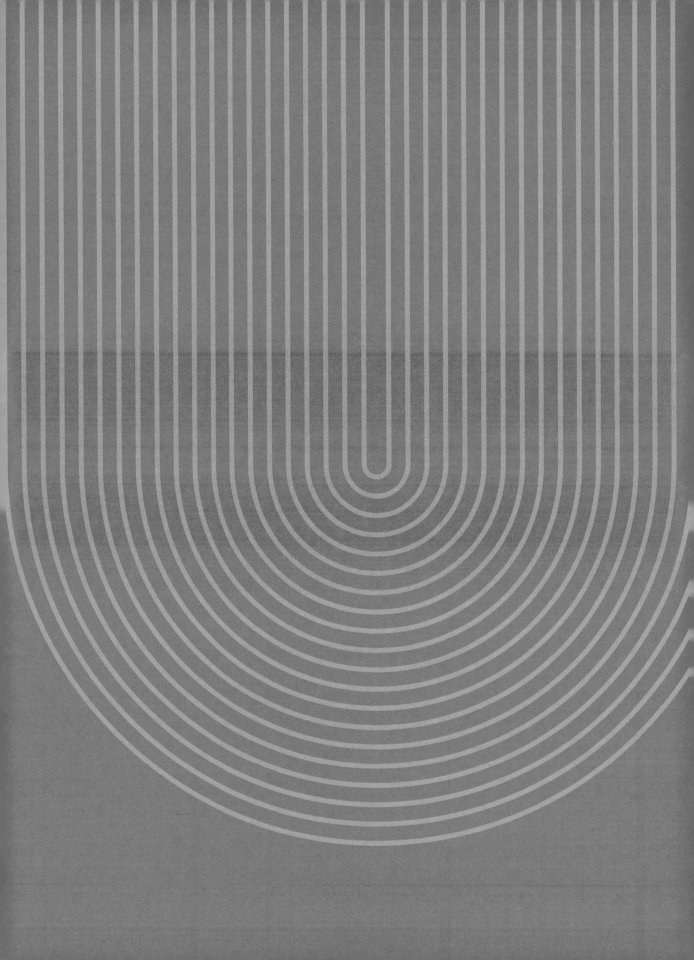

SLOW
STYLE
HOME

SLOW STYLE HOME

TAKE YOUR TIME,

USE WHAT YOU HAVE, AND

TRANSLATE YOUR VISION INTO A HOME YOU LOVE

ZANDRA ZURAW

Gibbs Smith

First Edition
29 28 27 26 25   5 4 3 2 1

Text © 2025 Zandra Zuraw
Photographs © 2025 as noted throughout

Published by

Gibbs Smith

570 N. Sportsplex Drive

Kaysville, Utah 84037

1.800.835.4993 orders
www.gibbs-smith.com

Designed by Sheryl Dickert
Printed and bound in China

This product is made of FSC®-certified and other controlled material.

Library of Congress Control Number: 2024941753
ISBN: 978-1-4236-6762-9

To Calvin and Quinn,
my hope is that our home has given you
the space to become the best of who
you want to be.

And to Pete,
for creating that possibility with me.

Contents

WELCOME TO SLOW STYLE

Experiencing and living with beauty is something everyone needs and deserves

Having a home we love, one that looks beautiful, functions well, and gives us energy and support is something that should feel attainable. If you feel your "dream home" is out of reach, then either your definition of a dream home is out of alignment with who you are or you've been bulldozed into believing you don't deserve it or can't afford it.

How did I come to believe this? How did I get to the point where I have an entire framework laid out to teach you how to create your own dream home using my Slow Style philosophy?

I'm not a professionally trained interior designer. And presumably, neither are you. There could be several reasons why you've picked up this book rather than hiring a designer. Perhaps you can't afford one. Maybe you just don't know how to find one who you'll be sure you can trust to understand what you want. Or maybe you want to embrace the process of creating your own style yourself. I fell into that last category when starting out, and I think that coming from that perspective is the best place to start using Slow Style.

Page 2: Photo by Erin Little.

Opposite: Design and photo by Natasha Habermann.

Above: Design by Zandra Zuraw; photo by Erin Little.

9

My first foray into developing my aesthetic started in my childhood bedroom. In a small closet with accordion doors, to be precise. I turned it into a New York City apartment. It would be several years before my first visit to that city, but somehow, I knew that I wanted a space to call my own and that I wanted it to feel efficient and private, meeting my needs and having my personality out on display, despite the limited wall space a closet provided. It turns out I've always made a connection between the development and expression of who I am with the concept of home.

Fast forward to my college bedroom, where I experimented, as many of us do, with self-expression. It was in a college course in art history that I first discovered the emotional power of encountering an oil painting in real life, rather than a reproduction. I searched out a poster in the gift shop for a particular painting that wasn't what everyone else was displaying (i.e. the obligatory Van Gogh or O'Keefe). I wanted to differentiate myself from my college roommates and, I suppose, feel special. As is common with most young adults, I was trying to figure out who I was, make my mark, and declare my individuality. I instinctively used the walls of my room as a way to do so.

After college came a series of apartments, first in New York City and then in Chicago. These years were dark ones for me as I first came to terms with clinical depression that I had been denying for several years. I had no idea what I wanted to do with my life, and I was trying to figure that out while beginning therapy and medication for my mental health. All throughout these years, my apartments were my places of refuge. I cared deeply about how they looked and felt. Every time I explored a new aspect of myself or followed my curiosity into a potential career path, little representations of those things would show up in my rooms. Sometimes it was a particular color I chose to paint a piece of furniture that I picked up on the side of the road. Another time, it was the first set of grown-up bowls I purchased at Crate & Barrel. As I floundered around in my career

path—pursuing graduate school in cultural anthropology and then social policy and holding a ridiculous number of jobs—I was developing my eye for design. That, at least, was a constant in my life, even if I didn't realize it then.

In my adult life, I've now lived in three homes. And, of course, with every move came the excitement of a new place to design. I'll never forget the moment I walked into my first home for the first time. My then boyfriend, now husband, had moved in ahead of me. We had found a late 1800s brick row home. At 1,600 square feet, it felt like a mansion to me, compared to the small apartments I had been renting. And the most special thing of all was that we had a tiny garden out back. We had almost no furniture yet, but my boyfriend had clipped a peony from outside and it was sitting in a glass bottle waiting for me when I opened the door. That small act of creating a beautiful moment out of what we already had at our fingertips was everything to me.

Skipping ahead many years and two children later, I finally succumbed to my obsession with interiors. I put it this way because, at first, I was a bit embarrassed about how much I loved wallpaper, light fixtures, and a weathered soapstone countertop. I knew there were big problems in the world and lots of people who didn't even have a roof over their heads, let alone the ability to decorate their spaces. So the delight I felt at seeing beautiful interiors somehow felt superficial and inconsequential. Eventually I realized that experiencing and living inside beauty is something that everyone actually needs and deserves. Once we've got our food, clothing, and shelter, and we aren't in danger of physical harm, then living through the daily grind of life and achieving happiness, at least in part, depends on experiencing beauty. And beauty doesn't have to have a hefty price tag. It might be living with a single potted plant, seeing and smelling a delicious meal in front of us, or lying down in well-loved linen sheets. As with the peony in the glass bottle, there are many small ways to create a beautiful environment.

Design by Zandra Zuraw; photo by Erin Little.

About fifteen years ago, I began the process of creating the life I'm currently living. This is a life where I've dedicated myself to teaching others how to create beautiful environments in which to live. To do that, I've had to deconstruct all of the steps I've taken to create my own version of a dream home and figure out what they are. Because I didn't start out with the intention of sharing my process with anyone, I really had to think about how my aesthetic has come to be. How did I learn the design principles used by the pros? How did I gain confidence in my color and pattern choices? How did I know when a particular furniture arrangement wasn't working and how to fix it? And how did I come to know the value of something at an antique fair? Or of a newly designed, to-the-trade piece of furniture for that matter? In an effort to tease apart the *how* of these questions, I started to build a teachable framework, which I've shared in this book.

WHAT IS SLOW STYLE?

Slow Style is an approach to creating a home that focuses on the *process* of interior design rather than the end result.

If you're familiar with Slow Food, you already have an inkling of what I mean by Slow Style. Slow Food started in Italy as a protest against the arrival of the first McDonald's in Rome in the 1980s. Journalist Carlo Petrini is widely accepted as the founder of the movement, which is now formally recognized across the globe. The focus of the Slow Food movement is to preserve the experience of an enjoyable meal, defined as a meal that employs methods of growing, harvesting, and cooking that are respectful and appreciative of one's cultural heritage. You can see why it started in Italy! Because all of these aspects have economic and geopolitical ramifications, Slow Food is seen as a response to all kinds of "fast" mechanization and mass production related to how we experience life.

As a side note, when I was searching for a profession, one of the things I studied was issues of food security, genetically modified crops, and the preservation of heirloom seeds in preparation for global food shortages. When I say my path to finding out what I wanted to do with my life wasn't a straight line, I'm not exaggerating! If you're in the same boat, you're going to love how Slow Style celebrates the many variations of how you become who you are.

In addition to Slow Food, the Slow Fashion movement, which has its roots as early as the 1960s and 1970s, came more to the forefront starting in the early 2000s. Slow Fashion focuses on how we design, manufacture, ship, and market clothing. When I say Slow Style in terms of design then, I am contextualizing this term in similar movements in food and fashion, emphasizing where we get our products from, how they're made, and how often we replace them. Slow Style also encompasses a more personal aspect: how we choose objects and give them meaning as part of a personalized aesthetic whose very purpose is to reflect who we are.

Design and photo by
Erica Swagler.

THE PHILOSOPHY BEHIND SLOW STYLE

As I looked back at the development of my own design aesthetic, the first thing I realized was that the pace of the development of my own signature style is, in and of itself, a key ingredient of the recipe. Going slowly with this kind of design is something you have to accept. That's because our style, our aesthetic is a continuous reflection of who we're becoming throughout our lives.

But perhaps to say that you must "accept" going slow is a misnomer. When you're fully in the practice of creating a beautiful, meaningful home, you aren't really aware that you're going slowly. You're simply in the moment, thinking about how you want to set up your mantel, arrange a room, or test out how the wall colors flow from one room to another. You're caught up in whatever you're currently working on and you're perfectly happy to be there. At least I am! And I want you to be, too.

So when I say you'll have to go slowly, what I really mean is that you *will* go slowly, or that you *get to* go slowly, whether you realize you are or not. Don't let that be discouraging. Have fun while you try out new things, seeing your vision come to life. Instead of thinking of a slow pace as tiresome, embrace it as the ideal way forward. You can still have a few big ta-da moments when

Opposite: Design and photo by Beth Diana Smith.

Left: Design and photo by Erica Swagler.

you do a whole room makeover and experience the thrill of looking at your before-and-after photos. Just know that this won't be the last time you redo that room.

Honestly, I think it should be a relief that we don't have to have everything "done" all at once in our homes. Many of us feel that pressure, especially when we move, whether it's downsizing or upsizing. If the reason we move is for an upgrade, we feel the need to see our dream home realized quickly and be exceptionally outfitted. After all, there's a whole TV network dedicated to creating fabulous looking homes, along with a huge industry behind our cultural obsession

with celebrity-designed interiors. And it all seems to happen overnight.

But those shows, those Instagram accounts, those magazine covers . . . they don't tell the whole story. And they aren't exactly mirroring reality. You don't have to take my word for it. I've interviewed many people who work on HGTV shows and magazines and they've all told me it's not real life. That's not to say that design and decor media can't be inspiring and motivating. I'm just saying that you can't use those photos as a blueprint for creating your home, or as a yardstick to measure how you're doing.

WHY USE THE SLOW STYLE APPROACH?

The following explains the benefits of using the Slow Style approach.

It's How You Master the Mix

You know that seemingly elusive "perfect" mix of furniture, objects, and accessories that some fabulously creative person has combined unexpectedly, but with a great amount of sophisticated taste? We all want that, right? When you create your aesthetic over time, you're opening yourself up to several experiences that will help you master the mix.

One is the opportunity for serendipity to take hold. Let's say you're working on a bedroom and you need bedside tables. We've all become trained by Google searches to use keywords, setting parameters

to narrow down our choices. It's great for some things. But for our homes and creativity, it immediately cuts us off from the possibility of finding a gem that we didn't even know existed.

First you type in "bedside tables." You get way too many to choose from! So you narrow it down by material (wood, marble, mirrored, and so on). Or you narrow it down by style (farmhouse, mid-century, cottage, and so on). Still so many choices! Now you feel overwhelmed. You decide to narrow it down to a price range. And this is where your perspective gets really manipulated. Your focus has shifted from looking for something that makes your heart happy to something that seems reasonably priced, but only in *comparison* to the other links Google is showing you. You're about to make a generic purchase. It might be "fine." It might do the job. But you're not helping yourself create a signature style.

The Slow Style approach keeps functionality of spaces, furniture, and objects in mind. It helps you know things like how much room you have and what height would be ideal and allows you to be open to finding unique options that you hadn't yet imagined. Instead of searching for a side table online, go thrifting or antiquing and maybe you'll find a vintage step stool with the exact amount of chippy paint you love that works perfectly as a side table. Look through what you already have. Maybe your grandmother's heirloom chest could be on one side of the bed. Or maybe when you're walking through a craft show this summer, you'll meet someone making beautiful furniture with an unusual mix of woods. Now you're composing a room that looks like none you've ever seen.

When we step into a room that feels beautifully layered, exudes character and charm, and represents the personality of the owners, we typically see pieces combined in unusual ways, from different periods, and different styles. These are rooms that have taken their sweet time to come into their own.

Opposite: Design and photo by
Angela Chrusciaki Blehm.

Left: Design and photo by Beth
Diana Smith.

Design by Trevor Fulmer; photo by Sabrina Cole Quinn.

It's Therapeutic

The Slow Style approach offers the opportunity for personal development. From time to time, it's useful to check in and ask ourselves if we're living the best life we can possibly live, as the best person we can possibly be. This is baked into the Slow Style approach whenever you look around your home and wonder if it's still serving you.

Are the colors, patterns, and objects still giving you a feeling of delight? Is the furniture arrangement facilitating the kinds of human interaction you want to have? Are the things you've hung on the wall still inspiring you? And are the materials you're sitting and sleeping on offering you deep comfort? To answer those questions, you'll also have to ask yourself if there are mental, emotional, or interpersonal blocks that are standing in your way. And the million-dollar question is—what do you think will make you truly, deeply happy at this time?

Our homes are the most logical place to do this kind of soul work. I'm not the most woo-woo person I know, but I do speak of the soul as the part of us that expresses both our truest feelings and values, as well as the part that represents our highest aspirations. When I say "soul work," I simply mean having conversations with ourselves, about ourselves.

It Helps You Spend Money Wisely

With the Slow Style approach, you will also experience the pleasure of no-regrets purchases, at least a lot more often than when you rush to fill up a room. Sometimes you'll pay more, but in those cases you'll do so because you've taken the time to save up for something you really, truly want. You'll have it with you for a lifetime rather than a measly five years, and you'll appreciate it every time you run your hand over it. Any number of happy moments will come from this: you'll remember the search itself, you'll remember the story of how you finally found the perfect piece, or

maybe you'll feel so happy you waited until you could afford something that was expertly made. No buyer's remorse.

On the other hand, you can also *save* a lot of money when you use the Slow Style approach. For one thing, you're going to get a handle on those impulse purchases when you're at Target! You know the ones . . . you go in, shopping for paper towels and aspirin, and you end up with a vase, a set of mugs, and a new doormat in your cart. (I've been there. Many times.) Slow Style requires you to stop and ask yourself questions about the product and reflect on what's actually missing in your home, if anything. You'll be able to resist the temptation to buy things you may not need or will regret later.

Design by Vestige Home; photo by Rebecca McAlpin.

Design by Rydhima Brar of Rterior Studio; photo by Pablo Enriquez.

When practicing Slow Style design, you'll also be saving money because you've opened yourself up to shopping at thrift, consignment, and antique stores. You've probably seen those videos where someone shows this amazing find they scored for pennies on the dollar. I promise, that can be you. I'm not saying you're going to be on *Antiques Roadshow* with a million-dollar find you bought for twenty-five bucks. But thrift, consignment, and antique stores will help you achieve an eclectic look, and for a lot less than what you'd pay to buy everything new, off the big-box shelves.

And let's not forget about using what you already have. This is always, always, always my first piece of advice when someone is stuck and doesn't know where to start. If you're thinking about a new rug, a chest of drawers, or a new chair, move things from one room to another and test out the different sizes and functions of things. You may find you like the new arrangement so much you don't need anything new. Or maybe you'll be thrilled you finally found a use for something you've had stored away. Doing this also allows you to become very sure of what's working and what's not. If you bring a chair into your bedroom that has been in your living room and start using it as a reading spot for your morning coffee, you may realize that it would be a whole lot more comfortable if you could stretch out your legs. Or maybe the chair is too big for the small corner you've got. Now you know with certainty how big a chair for that space should be or if you need an ottoman. You've got clarity on what to look for when you're finally ready to buy.

It Expands Your Understanding of the World

The fourth reason to use the Slow Style approach is the connection between you and the rest of the world. Slow Style means you can take your time to seek out materials, objects, furniture, and finishes that are sensitive to the impact of global supply chains, fair labor wages, and environmental pressures on our natural resources. Anything in our material world that is "fast"—whether it is fast food, fast construction, fast money, or fast education—usually comes at the expense of someone or something else. Quality, equity, and the health of people and our planet almost always suffers. By taking the time to thoughtfully consider all the choices we're making in our homes, we're putting the brakes on knee-jerk reactions and impulse purchasing that may have impacts we haven't considered.

At the same time, we're also giving ourselves the gift of learning about people and places different from our own, about the process of how things are made, about the stories behind the treasures we find. Following our curiosity keeps us young. To me, a Slow Style approach to design is a richly rewarding experience that fulfills me in a way that catalog and internet searches could never replace.

Design by Trevor Fulmer; photo by Sabrina Cole Quinn.

THE IMPORTANCE OF A SIGNATURE STYLE

Presumably, you picked up this book because you don't want a cookie-cutter home. You feel a need, deep within, to proclaim your individuality. You don't want to blindly buy into what corporations tell you about the concept of home. You're tired of seeing the same old house layout, the same old kitchens, the same old family rooms. I get it. I don't want that either.

The problem is you might not even know what questions to ask to get that one-of-a-kind look. Many people come to me and ask very specific questions about what curtains they should buy, whether or not they should go with a dark paint color, or what kind of kitchen design would be good for resale. In all these cases, they're nervous about investing in a choice that may not fulfill their dreams, so they want to get it "right." They're afraid of making expensive mistakes that also might cost them a lot of time and hassle. Naturally, these are valid concerns. But these aren't questions that have definitive answers.

Every choice you make in your home is dependent on multiple factors. The very fact that you have questions about how to work within your personal budget, timeframe, and space limitations tells you that no answer to a design dilemma will be one-size-fits-all. I can't tell you what fabric, paint, or countertop material to choose without knowing a lot about your lifestyle, the people or animals you live with, how and what time of day you use a particular room, and how you want that room to function.

More importantly, I'd need to know about your aesthetic leanings, your passions, your values, your personal experiences, your travels, your family history, and your goals for the future to really give you solid advice. These last categories are the ones most people don't think to consider. And they're definitely not talked about in the quick-fix world of design advice we see in the media (social or otherwise).

When you ignore these other descriptors of who you are, where you come from, and who you want to

Opposite: Design and photo by Beth Diana Smith.

Left: Design by Vestige Home; photo by Rebecca McAlpin.

Below: Ribbon artowrk, design, and photo by Angela Chrusciaki Blehm.

be, your style will never be singular. It won't ever feel truly connected to the one and only you. From now on, when I use the word *style* in relation to Slow Style, know that I'm talking about creating a *signature style* that's all yours. The most challenging aspect of putting the Slow Style framework into practice is wrapping your head around the idea that you can't make *any* design decisions without first having a vision for what you want to feel and experience in a particular room. That's the way toward a signature style.

In the next chapters, you'll read about the three principles on which I've based the entire Slow Style framework. Absorb them, think about how they apply to you in particular, and allow yourself to be open to a new definition of your signature style. Then, get started creating that dream home at a pace that feels right for you.

PART I

To help others create their dream homes, I wanted to lay a foundation that could be applied to any style preference, budget, or location. What information do you need, what are the steps you'll take, and how do you know you're making good decisions? Here are the three foundational principles of Slow Style that you can use to make a room work in terms of functionality, aesthetic, and personal reflection: Life Informs Style, Style Evolves, and Style Reflects Your Values.

In the following chapters, we'll break each of these principles down into actionable steps along with conversation and examples from some of my favorite Slow Style practitioners.

LIFE INFORMS STYLE

L ife informs style" means that how you see yourself, your past experiences, your current living situation, and your dreams for the future will all come into play when you make design decisions. In other words, what your dream home looks and feels like—and how it functions—is based on who you are, where you've been, and who you want to become.

FORM VERSUS FUNCTION

You've probably heard of the "form versus function" dichotomy. It refers to whether it's better to design something that's beautiful (form), even if it doesn't work properly, or if it's better to design something that works well (function), but sacrifices beauty. Let me start by saying that, in my mind, being practical is just as important as getting on with the pretty side of decorating. So in the form versus function debate, I say both things matter.

Opposite: Design by Katie Saro; photo by Kris Ellis.

Above: Paintings, design, and photo by Angela Chrusciaki Blehm.

Design and photo by Natasha Habermann.

Things to Consider Around Function

Function refers to how well spaces, furnishings, and belongings are working in your home, taking into consideration such things as the stage of life you're in, the square footage of your rooms, who you live with, your daily responsibilities and demands, your budget, and so on. You'll have to look at your space with an unbiased eye and determine what's not working and why. A family of five will have different functional needs than someone who lives alone. A house with pets is different than a house without them, as is a kitchen that works hard three times a day versus a kitchen that's the

landing spot for takeout and meal delivery services. This may sound obvious. And yet, we get stuck in ruts in terms of how we use our spaces, and those habits can keep us from seeing what's not working.

If your home is stuffed to the gills to the point that it's weighing on you (literally and figuratively), you may have to admit you have a problem letting things go. If you feel crazed in any part of your life, take a look at the level of disorganization that may be going on in your home and then do something about it, rather than hiding under the covers. If you're only truly comfortable in one particular spot, start questioning why the rest of

Design and photo by Erica Swagler.

We made the most out of this small back entryway by adding shelving for shoes (which we painted the same color as the walls for a more tucked-in feel), and lots of hooks for coats, backpacks, and so on. Photo by Erin Little.

your space isn't supporting you. I speak from personal experience in all of these areas. I'm not saying it's easy to make changes. I'm saying it's worth it.

Consider the way the rooms are laid out and the systems that are used to organize them. Both have to work for *everyone* who lives there. There are a few small instances when you might be able to "train" your partner/spouse/roommate/children the way you want things to be set up, but for the most part, you're going to experience less daily friction if you come up with a plan that feels natural and logical to everyone who's adopting it.

A natural and logical use of space is what we're aiming for in general when we say we want a place to function well. We want the removal of friction. If you walk in the door and you have to step over things, if you have to move things off the counter to prepare dinner, if you can't use an extra room because it's filled with junk, you've got friction. And when you have people over, if there's no place to put down a drink or sit comfortably for conversation, you aren't creating an ideal environment for human connection.

Sometimes kids and adults have to share space. In Erica Swagler's living room she's made room for her son's drum set. I think it actually adds a nice touch of character!

Photo by Erica Swagler.

So, what to do about all this? Oftentimes the solutions lie in creative problem solving. (We'll get to creativity in the next chapter.) You may need to rethink the floor plan or even rethink how you're using different rooms. Maybe you'll need a new organizational system that makes putting things away only one step, not five. Maybe you'll need to do a big clean out and sell or donate a lot of items. If you live with other people, it can be a bit more complicated when you start to reorganize spaces, because you'll need to get buy-in. But don't let that stop you from creating a plan to achieve a smoothly functioning home.

Here, Erica is using baskets (her preferred storage option) for kids' sports equipment.

Photo by Erica Swagler.

When there's conflict, the most common flash points arise around spending money, having different levels of tolerance for clutter, and one person valuing practicality while the other values aesthetics. The goal is to make things work well for everyone while still looking damn good! If you can get everyone to at least agree on that, you're likely to land on a winning solution.

This isn't a couples counseling book (and I'm certainly not qualified to give relationship advice), but I will say that if everyone isn't committed to listening to all points of view, and really trying to understand each other, you're probably not going to solve conflicts that come up. Sometimes all you need is a calm discussion about why you want certain things to be certain ways, and everyone will jump on board because they see it makes sense and feels right. Just be prepared for others to have their own ideas about what "makes sense" and why. Coming up with solutions together is usually the best way and most effective long term.

You also might need to dig a little deeper into the reasons why someone is so adamant about their position. Maybe it's not really about the choice of couch that's up for debate. Maybe it has to do with a concern about the future, or something related to how they see themselves that's at the core of the resistance. If there's a standoff and neither person can get onboard with the other person's perspective, start making compromises. In my opinion, agreeing that if one person *truly* hates something then it's no longer an option goes a long way to everyone feeling like they have a say.

This also isn't a parenting book. However, when I hear people say that they can't have a "nice" home because they have small children, it makes me incredibly sad. You deserve to get pleasure from your surroundings, no matter the ages of your children, and having children living in your home doesn't mean you have no choice but to live with garish plastic toys scattered all over the place. You may decide to keep valuable china inside a hutch rather than using it for after-preschool snacks, but getting your kids used to ordinary porcelain dishes rather than red, yellow, and blue plastic ones (that may leech chemicals, to boot) isn't such a crazy idea, right? If style matters to you, take the Slow Style approach and focus on making your organizational and storage options as easy to maintain as possible, while also looking beautiful—however you define that. Sure, you'll have to be diligent when you're first teaching your children how to care for things, but isn't that an important lesson? And to ease your anxiety, I think the whole image of a child wiping their chocolaty hands all over the couch is way overdone. It's not like it's a given that this is going to happen, and you could just as easily be dealing with wine stains as Cheetos dust.

Design and photo by
Natasha Habermann.

Things to Consider Around Form

Now let's get on with the fun part, the decorating! Most people say they want their homes to reflect their personalities. And yet in practice, people usually don't know how to do this, how to translate their lives into visual autobiographies. So before you jump right into shopping, you've got to flesh out the *vision* you have for each room in terms of what you want to experience there. And that vision will be based on some aspect of your life, hence *life informs style*.

This room reflects so much of Katie Saro's life *and* style. The shelves are full of books that are obviously riffled through and used quite a bit by a large family. There's a formality to the couch but not to the bookcases. And certainly not to the wonderfully absurd red duck-foot stool!

Photo by Katie Saro.

I don't mean to be too lofty or turn this into an exercise of bestowing deep meaning onto every lamp you own. What I'm saying is that rather than thinking of your furniture and accessories as individual purchases, have an idea of how they fit into a bigger whole, so you get that "cohesive" feeling that many of my students and podcast listeners say their homes are lacking.

Design and photo by
Natasha Habermann.

Design and photo by
Natasha Habermann.

Have you ever tried to tie things together in a room by dotting the same color around and still felt unhappy with the results? That's because the kind of beauty you're going for isn't just skin deep. If you use a design element (like color) that isn't connected to an overall vision, it won't give you that cohesion you're looking for. (Not to mention that starting with a shopping list of items to look for quickly leads to feeling overwhelmed with all of the choices out there for everything from doorknobs to window coverings. But that's an entire conversation of its own.)

The Slow Style framework asks you to do some soul searching *before* you begin decorating to uncover why you're drawn to certain aesthetic choices. Have an honest conversation with yourself (and hopefully, those you live with), about your core values and passions as well as what you want to experience—emotionally, physically, spiritually, and through your senses—in each room of your home. Dig into your memory bank for experiences where you felt things deeply and viscerally because those are going to be the foundation of everything from color palettes to the types of materials you want to sit on and hold in your hands. When you have a cohesive vision laid out for each space, you're going to know what kind of rug to get with much more confidence than you would have if you just did a Google search for "area rug."

The work of every designer is to translate an imagined experience into the colors, materials, patterns, objects, and furniture that make up a room. But you can train yourself to do this, too. It won't be intuitive for everyone. And you may not even understand why it's so important right away. But I believe that every well-designed space—by which I mean, a space that's both beautiful and meaningful—comes together because each decision is intentionally chosen with that emotional experience in mind.

THE PROBLEM WITH STYLE CATEGORIES

One of my core teaching tools is a worksheet I developed to help you connect the dots between how you want to feel and the design choices that will invoke those feelings.

This worksheet came out of my frustration with the seemingly universal acceptance of style "categories." We've been indoctrinated into the gospels of popular categories such as "shabby chic," "farmhouse," and "boho" from product manufacturers, stores, design books, HGTV shows, and magazine articles. Maybe you've also encountered "coastal," "English country," or "Hollywood glam." These categories are useful when you need a shorthand description of something. It can help us quickly imagine what kinds of colors and furniture and patterns a room might have based on the mutually agreed upon definition of that look that was created by someone with lots of influence in the design community.

The problem is that even for designers who were, for the most part, creating these aesthetics from scratch, once everyone started to copy it, it became watered down and generic. Things that the designers found over time through serendipity and layered together to create a one-of-a-kind space are now being replicated through mass pro-duction. It's become challenging to tell a flash-in-the-pan trend from something truly interesting that will stand the test of time.

The other challenge with committing to a singular category is that it can never fully encompass all of who you are. I understand the appeal. You want a cohesive look throughout your home. You want things to go together. You want a way to narrow down your choices. But then real life happens. You receive a gift that doesn't fit at all inside the delineated lines of your style category, and you don't know what to do with it. You've chosen all of your furniture and accessories based on a style category and then grow bored of it. Or, like many people I've heard from, you like a variety of style categories and you don't want to have to choose between them! In that case, maybe your style category is "eclectic," but then you have no idea how to pull together that look.

Opposite: Design by Katie Saro; photo by Rebecca Fougerousse.

Opposite: Design
and photo by
Katie Saro.

Left: Design
and photo by
Erica Swagler.

YOUR STYLE MASH-UP

The worksheet I referred to is called the "Style Mash-up." At first, I thought all that was needed was to recognize the various style categories one was attracted to and mash them together. But even this didn't help people struggling against the constraints of style categories. It didn't help someone know how to combine a hand-me-down from a great-aunt, a dining table found on the side of the road, and dishware from a wedding registry.

Realizing the Mash-up needed more work, I came up with a few different iterations. Instead of mixing predesigned style categories, I zoomed out and asked people to identify what they were attracted to across the board, not just in terms of interiors.

This worksheet gives you a guided, outside-the-box type of brainstorming session with the purpose of freeing your mind of preconceived notions about what makes for a "cohesive" space, or a "well-decorated" space, and allows your own, true preferences to come through.

On the next page, you'll see a copy of the worksheet that you can use to find your style mash-up.

Opposite: Design by Aldous Bertram; photo by Blake Shorter.

FINDING YOUR STYLE MASH-UP

Step 1: Who Are You?

Choose one of the following personalities that describes you best:

Airy You're easygoing and try not to get stressed by little things. You pay attention to whether adding new things to your home will make it harder to stay organized.

Natural You orient yourself toward nature. You want the "natural," "native," or "organic" version of things when it comes to food, clothing, and homewares.

Refined You appreciate the good things in life: a spa vacation, excellent wine and food, beautiful clothing, and custom furniture.

Passionate You're passionate about things that interest you. You get energy from being with other people.

Write down your answer.

Step 2: What Type of Room Are You Most Drawn To?

Elegant You like rooms with attention to detail that feel sophisticated. Simple color palettes and classic design appeal to you.

Cozy You are tactile and want soft things in your room that you can curl up with. You like deeply personal things in your space.

Playful You love rooms with color and pattern. You're drawn to spaces that are "over the top."

Unexpected Rooms with one-of-a-kind pieces give you a lot of pleasure. You enjoy mixing old and new as well as different styles.

Write down your answer.

Step 3: Where Do You Fall on the Scale?

Old vs. New

Do you prefer a modern, more contemporary look or love all things old?

1 = contemporary furniture, art, and décor (made in the last 20 years)

5 = an equal mix of old and new

10 = all antiques all the time

Write down the number where you fall on the scale.

Minimalism vs. Maximalism

How much color and pattern do you like? How much space around objects?

How much stuff, overall, do you like in your rooms?

1 = space around every object so you can see its shape

5 = a few purposefully showcased selections

10 = multiple layers of color, patterns, and objects

Write down the number where you fall on the scale.

Step 4: Mash It Up!

Write down your answers from each of the three steps above.

Then turn it into a sentence. This is your style mash-up!

For example:

Natural + Unexpected + 3 + 5

"My style is natural and unexpected with a minimum of antiques, and I do love to display my collections."

Refined + Cozy + 3 + 3

"My style is refined and cozy with a few antiques and using a good amount of space in my rooms around objects."

For the full version of the worksheet, go to slowstylehome.com/book.

STYLE EVOLVES

The second principle of Slow Style is "Style Evolves," which refers to the fact that because you are an ever-changing person, your style can and should evolve along with you. I'm giving you a guilt-free permission slip to let go of things that you don't love anymore, no matter where they came from. This is also the principle that speaks to the "slow" part of Slow Style, in that you have to accept (or rather *get* to accept and eventually embrace) the idea that decorating takes time. At least it does if you want that one-of-a-kind, personality-filled home that looks and feels like no one else's. The one that reflects *your* signature style.

The good news is that you most likely already have a wealth of things to draw from—things you've been living with, or things you've put in storage, that you're going to learn how to repurpose. And of course you're also going to be buying new things (and new-to-you things from thrifting and antiquing). Your home won't have that effortless, eclectic, stylish vibe if you buy everything at once. So, just breathe and relax into the idea that your sense of what style you like will evolve as you develop your signature style. And remember, there is no finish line because Slow Style focuses on the process rather than the end result.

In these photos (facing page and following page), you see the evolution of Erica Swagler's sofa. First, she reupholstered it in a plain white linen, allowing the silhouette to take center stage. Then she experimented with pattern by tucking a block print sheet into the cushion. When she eventually found a pattern she loved, she reupholstered the sofa again.

Photo by Erica Swagler.

Designs and photos this page by Erica Swagler.

CREATIVITY THE SLOW STYLE WAY

There's more to the principle of "Style Evolves." It also encompasses the act of being creative. Sure it's helpful if you feel you have a knack for design or a natural inclination to be creative. But even if you're already comfortable with things like arranging flowers, painting furniture, and laying out a beautiful table, you'll still want to allow your creativity to evolve through practice. That's where my belief that everyone can be creative comes from. The kind of creativity you really need for your beautiful, meaningful dream home can be learned because all it takes is practice, which anyone can do.

For one thing, you'll often employ creative problem solving, which is something you've likely done in some other area of your life. Every job requires it. Raising children requires it. Getting through school requires it. In your home, you may need to think through the best way to organize something, the best way to turn that random collection of ingredients in your fridge into a meal, the best way to make use of that awkward corner in a room. You can do these things! Many times you'll have to actually try out your ideas and adjust them if you find they don't quite work. You may not nail the solution on the first try. Hence, style *evolves*.

You'll also need to take time to educate yourself about why things work and why they don't, from a design perspective. For example, futz around with different objects on your mantel, putting a few things up there, stepping back and looking at it, and then pulling some off, replacing things, and moving them around. To learn from this exercise means taking the time to *notice* what happens when you change out one object for another. When you change the size of something, or the shape, or the height, or the number of objects, how does that affect the vignette as a whole? Tuck those lessons into your memory for future use. And then do it again.

In order to develop your eye for design, you must be willing to get hands-on. You'll have to move furniture around, swap out rugs and rehang artwork, paint a room a different color, and rearrange bookshelves. Learning by doing is, in and of itself, a way to practice creativity. Which is why I believe anyone can create their own signature style, if they're okay with letting style evolve.

Design by Trevor Fulmer; photo by Sabrina Cole Quinn.

On this and the facing page, designer Katie Saro plays around with furniture and lighting to create different compositions over time.

Photos by Katie Saro.

Design and photo by Natasha Habermann.

THE TEN-YEAR RUG EXPERIMENT

Here's an example of one of the ways my style has evolved over the years, and what I learned about design along the way. When we first moved into our latest home, I bought a rug based on two of the other main colors that were dominant in the room: our big red couch and an extra deep, blue upholstered chair. This is a very common mistake people make. It takes more than color to unify a room's design. And often, the thing you buy that matches the other colors of things you already own, is something you don't even like and wouldn't necessarily buy if you weren't trying so hard to align the color palette. This kind of purchase means the whole room leaves you feeling unsatisfied. I didn't particularly love the rug I bought. It had an almost childlike large floral pattern, with the flowers reminiscent of the simple daisy that so many kids draw when they're young. The large blooms were red and blue with little bits of yellow in the leaves, on top of a neutral field of creamy beige.

To give you the full picture of what was going on, I must confess that I had painted the walls a "strong" (read: garish) yellow color that totally embarrasses me now. In my defense, we were moving from a much larger home where I was really happy with our mustard yellow living room; I didn't realize that that color wouldn't translate into a much smaller room that had completely different natural light. Note to self: bringing along all of your half-used cans of paint to a new place is pointless. Lesson learned.

Anyway, I now had this very, very bold color scheme compounded by the fact that there wasn't a lot of visual breathing room in the space, and I thought I should at least tie the colors together with the rug. It was a mess, but I didn't realize all this right away. I had to live with it for a while. I needed time to observe more rooms that *were* working in order to understand that the wall and rug colors I'd chosen weren't enough to make this room feel cohesive.

A few years later, I was ready to paint the room. I chose a wall color that would now really show off the additional artwork we had been collecting, rather than compete with it. I also painted the adjoining dining room the same soft gray because I realized that the two rooms were too small to handle two different wall colors when you could clearly see into one from the other. I was also secretly pleased when a friend spilled red wine all over the rug, giving me an additional excuse to ditch it for something that reflected how my design was evolving. (Maybe you've had a similar hope that something in your home would be destroyed?)

By now, I was paying attention to flow, not just between the living and dining rooms, but all the way into part of the kitchen because the line of vision went through all three spaces. I decided a little bit of black in each room would ground all the colors, materials, and patterns I was using. In the kitchen, I painted the window seat, trim, and muntins black. I had recently scored big on Craig's List with a mid-century dining table and chairs and recovered the seats with a black squiggly pattern. And I started looking for a rug with black in it. I found a rug with a large scale, black-and-white chevron pattern from a modern furniture and home decor chain retailer. I really liked the look of it, and the chevron brought a lot of energy to the room. It felt zingy next to the more sober wood pieces. This rug completely changed the entire room, to the point where I'm not sure I had even realized how poor a job the other rug had been doing. So this solution worked for a little while.

The problem with this new rug, however, was twofold. First, it was trendy. Chevron was everywhere at the time, on clothes and bags and lampshades and wallpaper. I loved it. But it seemed to go out of style as quickly as it had come in. That's the problem with fads. It's often hard to know if something is a flash in the pan or if it has staying power. Rule of thumb, if a design is showing up everywhere from Paris runways to wrapping paper sold for a school fundraiser, it's probably not going to last. Another way to deal with fads is to buy something from the original trend instead of the new version. For example, if I had found a vintage flame stitch chevron rug, that wouldn't have felt as trendy as the chain retailer's version. I had learned another lesson.

The second problem with the new rug was that it started to lose its shape and look tired about a year after we bought it. Some pieces at chain retailers can be well made, but not this particular rug, apparently.

By this point, I had experienced several important design lessons. Let's recap:

- **Don't buy based only on color.** Buying a rug (or anything, really) based only on color for the purpose of tying other colors together, usually doesn't end well. You must love the thing itself—on its own—to make it a worthwhile purchase. Otherwise your room will still feel just as "off" as it did before.

- **How one room flows into another visually is important.** You want to feel continuity as you transition between rooms via the materials, patterns, colors, and so on.

- Beware of fads and question trends, especially for large investment pieces.

- **Quality matters**. A lot happens on a rug. You shift furniture around more than you might realize, and you walk all over it constantly. If you have kids or pets, compound that wear and tear by ten. A cheap rug is going to look cheap pretty quickly.

- **A rug has a huge impact on the overall feel of a room.** It defines the area in which something happens . . . a conversation, play zone, where you'll gather to watch a big game on TV. A floor presents a large plane of decorative opportunity and you need to make the most of it.

Design by Zandra Zuraw; photo by Erin Little.

And this is where my third and current rug came in. I now understood that a truly well-made rug can cost thousands of dollars. (And no, you can't get by with a smaller rug just because it costs less. The size of the rug is determined by the size of the room and the area it's defining in that room.) Once you understand how high-quality rugs are made, you'll understand the prices. So if you're on a budget like I was, you have another option: go antiquing.

At this point, I knew I wanted a high-quality rug made of 100 percent wool, and I didn't want it to have

a trendy pattern. I started noticing how many of the designers I admired used what's often referred to as "oriental" rugs, meaning rugs that have a specific type of construction and come from a few different countries including Turkey, Iran, and Afghanistan. I discuss these rugs and what to call them in a later chapter. For now, think of the old rugs your grandparents may have had. If you're worried your room will feel too formal, stuffy, or stuck in a time warp, don't. These rugs can be terrific foils for modern furniture just as easily as they fit into classical rooms. So, I started the hunt.

Luckily, I live near Brimfield, Massachusetts, where a huge antique fair is held three times a year. The fair offered ample stalls to browse, filled with these rugs. I was able to find a large enough rug with just the right amount of wear (not too much for my taste, but a little was totally fine). I hardly even considered the colors! With the last two rugs I bought, I was leaning hard on color, asking it to do the entire job of bringing the room—and then the whole house—together. I was learning that color is just one way to create cohesion, and it wasn't a tactic that appealed to me any longer. When I texted photos of the rug that I was considering to my husband he asked if I worried the red in the rug would clash with the red in our couch. I did not. It was the entirety of the rug that I was looking at . . . the weave, pattern, wear, size, era. The rug was a proven classic that I knew would ground the room, give it a feeling of history, staying power, and even gravitas. I got it for a song and was delighted with the way my style had evolved.

What does this long story have to do with creativity or being a creative person? Observation and practice. Train your eye for your own purposes so that you can create your dream home—that's what you have to do. Pay attention and practice your skills. You don't have to be born with a special creative gene. You simply must be willing to try something new, live with it for a bit, assess whether or not it's working, and then make adjustments as necessary.

PRACTICING CREATIVITY WITH VIGNETTES

You can practice these skills on a smaller scale much more often than you'd want to be changing out a rug! This is why I love vignettes. Taking a group of objects and assembling them in different ways builds your creative muscles and refines your eye. Think about still-life paintings. Often, these are a collection of objects that may have some thread of a relationship to each other, but more importantly, their shapes and materials come together in an aesthetically pleasing way.

I change up my vignettes regularly. In this one you can see my love of natural objects: a turtle shell, starfish, porcupine quills, ostrich eggs, and fan coral. Photo by Erin Little.

If ever you are in need of inspiration, just peruse the work of designer Sean Scherer. He's a master at creating all kinds of compositions. In the photos on page 49, you'll see four completely different vignettes of his, all against the same white wall.

A vignette is something you can do with what you already own; it doesn't take very long, you don't have to move any furniture around, and you can have fun while doing it. Simply clear off a surface somewhere in your home. Look all throughout your different rooms and grab a few of your favorite objects. These could be a book, bowl, lamp, old camera, tassel, postcard, shell, candle, scarf, vase, or even something utilitarian.

Then start playing around. Groups of odd numbers tend to be pleasing to the eye, as do a variety of heights. Think about shape. What does it look like to use only tall, skinny things versus a mix of tall, short, skinny, and wide objects? What does it look like to have all round things versus a mix of round, straight, and curved objects? What does adding a natural item do for the vignette? Think about materials. What happens when you add something with a bit of shine (like a mirror or brass candlestick)? And what does a mix of metals look like together? What about a basket next to something smooth? Try out different colors together as well as different shades of the same color.

If it helps, think about telling a story through these objects. How would you represent a favorite vacation? What about a hobby? What colors, patterns, and materials remind you of those things? Challenge yourself to get more abstract. How would you represent a childhood memory or a favorite meal? The objects don't have to make sense to anyone but you because the goal isn't for people to guess what your vignette is about. The goal is to practice putting objects together in an aesthetically pleasing way.

Design and photo by Sean Scherer.

Design and photo by Sean Scherer.

Design and photo by Sean Scherer.

Your Turn

To get you started, here's a step-by-step example of how I've created a vignette while noticing certain design choices. You'll see how height, shape, and visual weight all come into play.

1. *Decide on an inspirational starting point.* It could be a particular object whose color, shape, or material you love, and you'll choose your other items based around it. Or it could be a recent family vacation and you'll gather up some of your mementos. My inspiration for this vignette is simply seasonal. In this case it's spring and I'm using my collection of vintage ceramic birds.

Opposite: Photo by Sean Scherer. Above: This series of creating a vignette was photographed by Erin Little.

2. *Start working on the overall structure.* I always prefer using odd numbers. In this case, I wanted your eye to go up and down as you looked across the horizontal line of the bookcase, which is why I chose to put the birds in this order. I emphasized the difference in heights even more by putting two on stacks of books and one on a wooden spool.

3. *Adjust for visual weight.* Visual weight refers to how "heavy" one side looks in comparison to the other in your vignette. In that last photo, you see it was fairly well balanced because the bird on the far right was propped up on two books, while the bird on the far left was standing on only one. But I decided to take it one step further and not be so obvious about the largest bird having the heaviest visual weight. So I added a few vertical books over on the right. Doing that also breaks up the horizontal plane going across the tops of the birds' heads. In keeping with the spring theme, I used some of my vintage gardening books.

4. *Consider your mix of materials.* Ceramics are predominant in the vignette. Paper (books) is secondary. I had only one wooden item (the spool), so I decided to play with that a bit more by bringing in two additional wooden items. One was a hand-carved child's puzzle in the shape of a duck made by my husband's grandfather. The other was a greenhouse ornament, which I display every spring.

5. *Add your final touch.* At this point, the height, shape, scale, and visual weight of the vignette was looking good. But it needed some life. My final touch in many of these projects is to bring in a little nature. I filled the vessels with floppy chamomile and button flowers to give the entire arrangement some movement.

Even though I've numbered these steps, I don't want you to think it's an exact recipe that must be followed in order. You'll futz with height, color, scale, and so on, a few different times, mixing up the order as you go. Just start playing! You could even snap a few pics as you go along and then scroll through them to help you discern which arrangement you like best. Training your eye is all about trial and error, and creating a vignette is a no-risk way to start.

Design and photo by Sean Leffers.

STYLE REFLECTS YOUR VALUES

S o far, I've covered the first two principles of Slow Style: my assertion that "Life Informs Style," or in other words your style comes from your story, and that "Style Evolves," meaning you have to actively practice certain design skills to bring that story to life. Once I started teaching these two things to people, it became increasingly clear that the impact of our design and decor choices are felt beyond the walls of our homes. The third principle of Slow Style, "Style Reflects Your Values," connects your developing story to something larger.

Before diving into the key elements of this third and final principle, let me back up and share how I see this from a 10,000-foot view. What do I mean by "values"? Values can and do refer to everything from interpersonal values such as being kind and respecting boundaries, to spiritual values if any kind of metaphysical or religious practice is important to you, to ethical values regarding labor and natural resources.

Starting with this broad definition allows us to talk about how our values are going to show up in our homes in both big and small ways. Because whether you realize it or not, what you choose to bring into your home and hang on your walls reflects what you value in life. How you care for and organize your things reflects what you prioritize. And what you choose to buy is connected to a vast supply chain that goes around the world.

Sometimes our values are felt through small gestures. If you value graciousness, for example, you may pay particular attention to how you set up your guest room. If you value human connectedness, you may give a lot of thought to how your furniture is arranged for intimate conversations or large parties. If you value family time, you may have space inside and outside your home that easily accommodates certain activities.

Other interpersonal values may come up in your home such as how you decide to raise kids, nourish intimate partnerships, and interact with extended family. Although these things initially may seem unrelated to design, it's always worth taking a moment to ask yourself if there's some kind of connection between your values and how your home is set up. This includes furniture arrangements, organization, what your rooms are dedicated to, and so on. What you choose to hold on to, especially as it relates to hand-me-downs and heirlooms will also reflect what you value, and more importantly, will influence how you decide to use or display these items.

If you value your spiritual life or personal growth, you may have a space set up for prayer, meditation, yoga, or journaling. It can be just a small corner you've carved out or an entire room. You might have objects around your home that reflect your beliefs. You may have a shrine set up in remembrance of someone that includes religious artifacts, or a sanctuary that's for motivational purposes to keep you on track with personal goals. How privately or publicly you choose to share these values will be different for everyone.

In this living room by Rydhima Brar, the TV is off to the side, perhaps signaling that the family values both conversation and art. There is also room made for children without sacrificing the family's personal aesthetic.

Photo by Frank Francis.

Style Reflects Your Values

Values are also expressed through what we spend our money on (and what we don't). Because this is a book about design, the items that we spend money on for our home will be front and center. Decorating our homes often means making purchases. And while I'm going to encourage you to use what you have before buying anything new, the reality is, you're going to be spending money on your home, one way or another. This book will help you learn to align your spending with your values.

THE IMPACT OF THE DECORATING INDUSTRY

I referenced the Slow Food movement in an earlier chapter. The point of that movement is that natural, chemical-free food grown locally and eaten according to seasonality is best for natural resources, farmers, continuity of culture, and pretty much anyone who eats food. In retracing my steps from where I am today back to where I was thirty years ago when I first started to learn about design, I've come to realize that there is a similar ripple effect to how we decorate our homes. What we buy, where we buy it, who makes it, how it's made, and what we do with it when we no longer want it . . . all of these steps of acquisition have an impact beyond our own four walls. I don't think we can, in good conscience, decorate as if that impact doesn't happen.

Now please hear me when I say I don't believe in guilting or shaming anyone into becoming the poster child for ethical shopping. I'm not suggesting anyone should wear their ethics as a badge of honor for all to see and admire. And I certainly don't think any-one is better than anyone else when it comes to how they practice whatever ethical code they're living by. So please don't feel you have to defend yourself. I'm simply saying that becoming aware of the marketing, manufacturing, and distribution processes that are embedded in all that we own is a principle I adhere to, as best I can. If we really do want to slow down in many aspects of our lives, and slowing down is part of what drew you here in the first place, knowing how things are made and what they're made of is a critical part of that process.

If the goal, then, is to become more aware of the impact we're having when we shop for decor, then I'd like to have a term to define that effort. I struggled to come up with something, and I've landed on "ethical sourcing." This seems broad enough to cover multiple "best practices" in the environmental-socioeconomic landscape.

Design and photo by
Erica Swagler.

THE CHALLENGE OF ETHICAL SOURCING

Some companies focus on one or two very specific eco initiatives, while others are taking into consideration multiple environmental concerns at a more basic level but that allow them to still stay in business. In other cases, companies are focused on making sure the people on the production side have safe and healthy work environments and are paying people a living wage. Still other companies give back to their communities through philanthropy or by allowing employees to volunteer during work hours. It's unlikely that any single company is going to be "all ethical, all the time." You'll have to weigh what's important to you most, what you can afford, and what actually works in your home and for your lifestyle when choosing companies to buy from.

Natasha Habermann has a Roger + Chris green leather Chesterfield sofa in her library.

Photo by Natasha Habermann.

I want to be realistic as well as honest with you. Not everything you buy is going to be ethically sourced. And not everything I buy or own is, either. Sometimes the issue is the expense. Better made things, produced in ways that are fair to people and the environment, can be more expensive. The Slow Style response to that is to live with a placeholder (one that you still like, maybe one you've thrifted or that's a hand-me-down), until you can afford something new that reflects your values.

I wish we all had access to and could afford everything in our homes to be ethically sourced. But even if we did, there would still be debate about which particular ethical practice does the least harm. I'm not saying I have the answers. I'm sure I'm going to leave out some critical pieces of research on the environmental or socioeconomic effects of one approach over another. But I also don't want the complexity of the issue to paralyze my decision making. I want to try to do the least amount of harm in my own small way. And that's all most of us can do, right? One small thing after another, with limited time to do our own research.

I also think it's important to say here that the truth is, it's not always that we can't afford something, but that we're choosing to use our discretionary funds in different ways. Whether it's annual spending on mocha lattes or the decision to take a big vacation, we are all making financial decisions with the money we have. I think we've just become so used to less expensive versions of furniture and homewares, we balk at something that's price tag actually reflects its inherent value. I'm not saying everyone can or should buy $7,000 lamps. What I am suggesting is that you consider paying for the highest quality you can afford once you've determined the price makes sense based on how it's made, what it's made of, and how much you love it.

WHAT TO LOOK FOR

In this chapter, I will humbly put forward my take on what to pay attention to in the decor industry to help you navigate the myriad choices out there when it comes to buying things for our homes. The first thing I do when learning about a new company is go to their "About Us" page and see what they're saying. It can tell you a lot about what they value, sometimes overtly, and sometimes because of what they *aren't* saying.

Commitment to Craftsmanship

Later on in the book, I talk about "handmade" with a lower case "h." Right now, I'm talking about supporting the work of professional craftspeople with fair wages and safe work-places. When we value craftsmanship, we understand that years of experience and the transfer of expertise to younger generations is why you'll probably see a higher price tag on an item. Let's delve a little deeper into this idea.

Labor is often the most expensive part of the cost of producing goods. We've become so used to cheaply made accessories and furniture for our homes that we forget about why they're so cheap in the first place. One reason is unethical working conditions for those who are making these products. When you see a piece of furniture that costs more than a mass-produced counterpart, and there's evidence that some aspect of the product is handmade, that raises the likelihood that the process of creating that piece of furniture has been slowed down enough to value the work of the craftspeople.

Ted Bradley handcrafting ceramic rings that will become his signature light fixtures. I prefer to call them light sculptures because they really are works of art. Photo courtesy Ted Bradley.

I don't mean to ignore the reality of exploited workers who are doing things by hand and getting paid an abominable wage. But companies that make and sell these products don't usually put "handmade" front and center on their websites. If artisans are paid a fair, living wage—especially when carrying out a long-standing tradition of a particular craft—the company is going to be proud of that and want to share their stories with you. It's not always easy to fact check these things, but the number of items produced by a certain company and the prices they charge can be an indicator.

Sensitivity to Environmental Impacts

When at all possible, look for signs that a company has been thinking about the entire "cradle to grave" life cycle of their products. This means considering the environmental impacts of how natural resources are cultivated and the amount of energy used in production and transportation. It also means considering the time it takes for materials to decompose once they are discarded. On this last point, products made with natural materials (wood, cotton, wool, linen, stone, clay, and so on) typically cause less harm to our soil, water, and air than products composed of man-made materials and treated with toxic chemicals.

When you buy home goods that are produced from raw materials that are closer to where you live, you limit the amount of pollutants emitted into the environment through transportation. Find out a little bit about the natural resources found where you live, and then you can look for labeling that will tell you either where the product is made, or where the materials are from, or both.

I realize that not all of the materials our products are made from are going to come from where we live. The environmental cost of transportation has to be balanced with availability of the materials themselves, and how renewable they are in terms of regrowth. For example, a big reason we chose to use bamboo flooring in our kitchens is because of how quickly bamboo grows. It's a natural resource that can be easily replenished, although the downside is that it has to be shipped across the world to get to us in the United States. As I said earlier, there aren't perfect solutions, so you will have to make decisions on a case-by-case basis.

Wallpaper "Maidenhair" in the Primrose colorway, by Fine & Dandy Co. Photo by Lasse Møller Jensen.

Protective Health Measures

Technically, anything that isn't safe for us to ingest is "toxic." The paint industry has grappled with this for decades, starting with the discovery that even trace amounts of lead from chipped paint picked up by infants was causing major problems in brain development. For almost fifty years, lead paint has been banned across the United States and in the last decade or so you've probably noticed paints advertised as "low VOC" or "zero VOC." You know those headaches you get when you're painting a room? They're caused by Volatile Organic Compounds, which are carbon-based compounds released as gasses, polluting not only our indoor air but the ozone layer as well. The really troubling thing about VOCs in my mind is that adverse health effects can last long after the paint has dried. My advice is to always go with zero VOC paint options to avoid the risk of adverse effects to your liver, kidneys, and lungs.

Wall paint "Meet Cute" by Clare; design by Orlando Soria; photo courtesy Clare Paint.

Wallpaper "Audubon" in the Alabaster colorway, courtesy Fine & Dandy Co.

Paint isn't the only place you'll find microscopic elements containing things we shouldn't be breathing. Have you ever had a new mattress or upholstered piece delivered to your house and smelled something really unpleasant? That's "off-gassing," which means the fabric and/or cushion inserts have chemicals in them that are releasing into the air and causing problems for our lungs; irritating our eyes, nose, and throat; and triggering allergies. Either the materials themselves are made with some form of plastic or they've been chemically treated.

Anything printed with ink is something to consider as well. Look for wallpaper and fabrics printed with plant-based inks (rather than petroleum-based inks) to avoid emission of ozone and/or mercury into the air. The truth is that a lot of products we bring into our homes have VOCs that should give us pause. Everything from cleaners and disinfectants to finishes on our floors and fabrics. If you're in an older home, you might actually have less indoor air pollution because, ironically, older homes are typically not as well insulated or tightly sealed as newer homes. If you're going to the trouble of maximizing your energy efficiency—which is great for the planet and your wallet—by sealing up all of those drafty nooks and crannies, please don't sacrifice your health by also sealing in gasses that pollute your indoor air!

These three aspects of the decor industry (commitment to craftmanship, sensitivity to environmental impacts, and protective health measures) are often intertwined. You can see how they are connected and how a company manages and values these concerns when you dig just below the surface of their homepage.

WHEN THE PRICE TAG IS WORTH IT

Keeping all the above in mind, here are some of my favorite value-driven decor products.

Area Rugs

Let's start with rugs. I am forever imploring people not to choose a rug as an afterthought. Especially when you're redoing an entire room at once, a rug seems to be something that gets less respect—and a smaller proportion of the budget—than furniture. But a rug is so important to the overall feel of a room! It can offer a foundation to build from (in terms of how you choose your other design elements); it can be a focal point (especially if the other items in the room are understated); or it can be the element that makes the entire room feel cohesive.

I won't sugarcoat it, though. New, well-made rugs are expensive, in large part because they are often hand-woven or hand-knotted and use all natural materials rather than synthetics. Countries located from Morocco and across North Africa, through Turkey, Iran, Afghanistan, and down into India, Pakistan, and Southern China are all places where generations of people have been passing down the intricate skills of rug weaving and hand knotting. Today there are companies collaborating with artisans from across the "Rug Belt" countries to produce their designs.

Rather than buying new, I often pick rugs up at antique fairs or shops because I like classic designs, and they are usually more affordable. You can tell if a rug is handmade by flipping it over. If it's a flat weave rug (made on a loom, without knots), the same pattern will be seen on the back as on the front. A synthetic, machine-made rug will often have the design printed onto the front. If it has any kind of pile (think of rugs that feel good underfoot from low-pile to shag), you want it to be hand-knotted. On the backs of these rugs, a machine-made one will look obviously uniform and precise because they aren't actually using knots to

Design and photo by Katie Saro.

make the rug, but a machine stitch instead. If you see slight variations in knot size on the back, you know it's been handmade.

If you're looking for an unused, contemporary aesthetic, I'm really taken with the rugs I've seen from interior designer Trevor Fulmer, who draws his patterns by hand and then works with traditional weavers in Nepal and India to have them produced. The weaving takes three people two-and-a-half months, which equals about 400 hours per weaver. That doesn't include the spinning and dyeing of the wool or finishing and stretching of the rug after it's woven. From spinning and dyeing wool, to weaving, washing, and stretching it, an eight-by-ten-foot rug with 100 knots per square inch (kpsi) typically takes a team of weavers three months of work. These rugs are made to last for generations, and I believe the designs will be timeless. Drawing his inspiration from the organic shapes found in nature means the rugs marry with other styles effortlessly.

A handwoven rug designed by Trevor Fulmer, part of his "Foundations" collection exclusively through Landry & Arcari. This is "etched" in the color fern.

Photo by Sabrina Cole Quinn.

Furniture

Like rugs, furniture will last longer when it's made with hardwoods (not plywood or other composites masquerading as hardwood), and when there haven't been shortcuts taken in the sewing and upholstery work. A piece of furniture won't feel lightweight if it's made of hardwood; fabrics should be made of natural materials that haven't been treated with chemicals. Buy the best quality you can afford for your biggest pieces so that you get decades of use out of them, rather than having to replace things every five years. Go with timeless styles, by which I mean ones that have been around the block and reimagined a few times. These will look good when paired with pretty much any aesthetic because they're naturally pleasing to the eye, comfortable, and useful in terms of size and shape.

I'm a bit obsessed with Roger + Chris, a company making sofas, sectionals, sleepers, and ottomans. I don't think there's an aspect of the values I've mentioned that they don't adhere to. Their hardwoods are cultivated in North America, and they replant trees in partnership with the One Tree Planted organization based on what they harvest. Every aspect of their furniture is handmade, from the frames to the upholstery, and they pay talented craftspeople a fair wage in their one and only production facility located in North Carolina.

On the eco-friendly side of things, there are no fungicides or pesticides used in the lumber (this is another benefit of not using raw materials transported from other countries); and the fabrics, cushion foam, and leathers are all made with such natural materials as organic wool and cotton, non-synthetic latex derived from rubber trees, and a chrome-free tanning process for leather. If you're an animal lover, they offer down and feather-free cushion fill and vegan "leather" fabrics.

Two process shots from Roger + Chris (one frame-related, one upholstery-related). Photos courtesy Roger + Chris.

Here's what I've learned from Roger + Chris about what to look for when assessing the quality of an upholstered piece:

- **The frame:** You want the entire frame to be solid wood, no composite woods that have been glued together. It should feel as heavy as it looks. If you pick it up by one corner, the other corner on the other side should easily come up with it, letting you know the frame isn't bending or sagging. The construction is most sturdy if the sides use dowels for joinery rather than glue, nails, or screws.

- **The guts (i.e. the suspension):** When you lift up the seat cushions on a sofa, you want to see either hand-tied springs with a little bit of room between them, or a tight array of lots of springs. If you see wide webbing on anything bigger than a chair, it will start sagging sooner than if you have coils. And if you see nothing at all other than a piece of fabric stapled to the frame, you're going to regret it.

- **The pillows:** Are the inserts made of high-density foam or polyfill? When you squeeze the pillow, the more resistance you feel, the better. This indicates the cushion will have less sag over time.

- **The fabrics:** Upholstery weight is a given, which simply means if you tried to make a fitted dress out of it, it would feel heavy and not compliant around your curves. Check on your options. There are eco-friendly, spill-proof options and stuff that's been sprayed with chemicals. The former won't off-gas, which is that awful smell that comes from a new sofa as soon as you take off the plastic wrap when it's delivered. If you want leather, make sure it's the real deal and not "leather bonding," which is the equivalent of buying a steak versus a hot dog with questionable ingredients. Or you can go vegan.

- **The stitching:** Handmade is best, especially if you've got some kind of tufting. (Those are the little buttons that pull the fabric toward them, all over the sofa or chair back. Or "channel" tufting, which is like wide fabric ribs, usually going vertically.)

Roger + Chris aren't making case goods . . . yet. But I hope they do in the future. (Case goods are what designers and furniture makers call things like dressers, buffets, and desks.)

Furniture by Roger + Chris; photo courtesy Roger + Chris.

Wallpaper and Paint

If you want a lot of bang for your buck when it comes to creating an atmosphere, wallpaper and paint are the way to go. You'll always want these choices to be part of your overall vision for what you want to feel and experience in a room. When thinking about your walls, consider how much art you have and how much you want it to stand out against the backdrop. The more art I have—especially really important pieces as opposed to thrift store finds—the more I go toward a smaller repeating pattern, possibly in a neutral color for wallpaper. If I'm just painting the wall, I want the artwork to be enhanced by the color, not competing with it. Notice I didn't say I'd want a totally neutral wall. A rich, deep brown or eggplant can be an amazing backdrop for artwork as much as a lovely cream. It really depends on the artwork itself and the kind of natural light you have in the room.

I love the ethos of the wallpaper company Fine & Dandy Co. So many of their designs are nature-inspired, and they take their responsibility to protect nature seriously. For their residential grade applications, the printed paper is made of 31 percent post-consumer recycled content that doesn't release any toxins into the air. The paper backing is 100 percent recycled content. By digital printing their papers with LED-cured inks, less energy is consumed in the production process. And because these inks are plant based, there are little to no concerns about toxins being released while the ink is drying in the factory or hanging in your home afterward. Finally, they recycle their unused ink as an eco-friendly way of trapping gasses and reusing the material inputs.

Mural "Zanzibar" by Fine & Dandy Co.; photo by Xie Yujie Nick.

Wallpaper (repeating pattern) "Morse" in the Citron color way by Fine & Dandy Co.; photo by Taylor Simpson.

Wall paint "Headspace" by Clare; design by Ashley Whiteside; photo courtesy Clare Paint.

Are you the type of person who needs to buy ten sample-sized paint jars and paint swatches all over your walls to find your perfect color? If this is *not* your idea of a fun Saturday, my suggestion is to trust the color expertise of Nicole Gibbons, designer-turned-CEO of Clare paint. Her primary mission is to make the color choosing process as painless as possible because this is where people often start to feel overwhelmed. If you go into a traditional paint store, there will be more shades of white than any normal person could possibly decipher. To simplify, she makes a careful selection of color within an essential number of palettes, and offers large peel-and-stick swatches to avoid having to use actual paint. Another thing I love about Clare is that her paints have zero VOCs. I think I've made it pretty clear why this is so important, for human and environmental health.

Wall color "Dirty Chai" by Clare; design by Ruthie Jackson; photo courtesy Clare Paint.

Ted Bradley's ceramic rings, lit from within and hung vertically. Seen here "Series," suspended from the ceiling.

Photo courtesy Ted Bradley.

Lighting

What really turned me into an advocate for quality craftsmanship was simply learning about how things are made. When we get to peek behind the scenes and see what goes into these products we begin to understand their value. Ted Bradley's lighting company is one such example.

I can't emphasize enough what a difference lighting makes in how a room functions and feels. Once you've figured out how many pockets of light you want, and how many purposes your fixtures need to fulfill, you'll want to think about the aesthetic of the lamps themselves. I've met and admired the work of sculptors and potters for years but had never met someone who was sculpting light the way Ted does.

It took him hundreds of iterations to perfect his perfectly circular porcelain rings that surround the LED bulbs he uses. What he was creating had never been done before and even the most experienced ceramicists he talked with told him it just wasn't possible. What Ted wanted was to completely enclose a strip of lights inside a ceramic ring so that the lights themselves wouldn't be visible. The rings would appear to glow from within. Each failed attempt represented days of work, hand-building ring after ring, using over 1,000 pounds of clay. It took a year to perfect the process. He doesn't see those days as losses, however. He sees them as pieces of the story that goes into handmade goods. He now has a team of four working with him, and each ring takes five hours to complete.

His inspiration comes from the natural world and an attempt to capture a moment of evolution in time. For example, his very first design was an abstraction of a whale skeleton bleached in the sun. To me it represents both a whale's heft and grace. We feel awe toward a creature so much bigger than we can imagine, as well as delight in how it glides, almost weightless, in the water. Since then, he's created other light sculptures as well, all with the same ethereal quality. Another favorite of mine is the one that looks like jugglers' rings, tossed in the air and suspended in time. You may have to save up to acquire one of these pieces, but owning a functional piece of art of this caliber and knowing how it's made is a great story to share.

I've shared just a smattering of companies putting craftsmanship, the environment, and our health at the forefront of their work. In each case, I've interviewed the people who've started these companies, which is how I came to know them. My hope is that in sharing stories of businesses who live their own values, I am confirming that there are ways to represent personal values you might hold, like ethical sourcing, in the products you buy. And hopefully this will get you thinking about your own values and how they're showing up (or not) in your home.

The original fixtures "Samsara" (above) and "Swag" (right) by Ted Bradley. Photos courtesy Ted Bradley.

PART II

My goal is to challenge the status quo when it comes to how we decorate and to inspire you to use the Slow Style approach as you make decisions about your home. Play with mixing things from different eras and design styles; create intentional areas for conversation, restoration, and experimentation; compose vignettes that tell stories; and figure out organizational systems that actually work to keep your clutter at bay. Sometimes the best way of explaining how to do something is to see it in action.

In the second part of the book, you'll see how Slow Style plays out in different kinds of homes. The chapters are divided into five main design elements that you'll see in every Slow Styled home: Antiques, Art, Nature, Handmade, and Heritage and Culture.

You'll see how these elements are incorporated by different designers, in different types of homes with a variety of aesthetics. Get ready to be inspired!

ANTIQUES

Every room should have at least one antique

There are plenty of people out there who don't need to be convinced that antiques and vintage pieces are wonderful things to include in their homes. So first, let me speak to those who really feel antiques aren't for them.

Usually, these folks are much more excited by contemporary design. It simply appeals to their general aesthetic. They don't like rips, scratches, or peeling paint because they appreciate furniture that's in excellent condition. They don't want someone else's dusty stuff from a great-aunt's attic. Sometimes they're minimalists who appreciate clean lines, unfussy detailing, and streamlined living. And sometimes they're

maximalists who are thrilled by metal, glass, and honed stone rather than old wood, Oriental rugs, and worn leather. Maybe they're the person in the group who's always checking out new technology—or philosophically, they want to look forward rather than back.

None of these things are wrong or bad! And if you fall into this category, you certainly can have a Slow Styled home. You're just going to be over on the "fewer" end of the old/new continuum than the "more" end. (Check out the worksheet in the first part of the book if you don't know what I'm referring to.) Because even you, my dear anti-antiques home lover, will benefit from at least one antique in each room.

Design and photo by Angela Chrusciaki Blehm.

Neither of these rooms feel like they came out of your great-aunt's Victorian attic, but they both do have vintage items in them. In Angela Blehm's contemporary living room (previous spread), the lamps are vintage, and in Rydhima Brar's modern era basement, she's added an '80s era lamp and a vintage Mies van der Rohe leather chair.

Photo by Mike Carreiro.

WHAT ANTIQUES DO FOR A ROOM

Antiques represent the fact that our lives are not lived in separate moments, unconnected to one another. If you look through your own Instagram profile or your library of Facebook photos, it may seem that way: a series of clicks capturing a single second in your life, usually the times when you're at your best or doing something "special." But that's not our lived experience. In addition to the celebrations, vacations, and really great dinner parties, there are the quiet moments—the moments when nothing major is going on, when we're just driving our car to the grocery store, doing the dishes, picking up our kids from band practice, getting dressed for another day at work, or riding the subway across town. These moments may not be exciting, but we all need to figure out a way to live through them, and even—dare I say—appreciate them. Otherwise, we'll just be chasing the next dopamine hit, which is why trying to keep up with decor trends is a slippery slope toward a feeling of never-enough.

Antiques remind us that people before us had lives full of excitement mixed with lots of "meh" moments. Some stand as a testament to the beauty of the everyday for the simple reason that they're still around. Others remind us that exquisite details can elevate us out of the everyday with fanciful flourishes that can make us feel like kings and queens inside our more humble settings.

Bedroom and photo by Erica Swagler.

Design and photo by Sean Leffers.

Antiques have stories within their materials. This is especially true because they come from a time when there were far fewer trends to chase, and the trends that there were lasted at least a decade rather than a month. There's a story of how an antique piece was made, the materials it was made from, and the circumstances under which the piece was acquired. Maybe it was built by someone in the family. Maybe it was something the family saved up for. Maybe it was a generous and thoughtful gift.

Design and photo by Sean Scherer.

Then there's the story of how a piece was used. Oftentimes, the reason it existed no longer applies to contemporary life. But when you reuse it in a different way, you're creating a new memory track within your mind because you think of both the old way and the new way when you look at it. And it makes you smile. Or makes you feel satisfied that you've had a creative epiphany about how to reuse it. These memory tracks are what give the day-to-day moments of life meaning.

Erica Swagler repurposes a dresser for storage and extra counter space in her kitchen.

Photo by Erica Swagler.

HOW TO INCORPORATE ANTIQUES INTO ANY ROOM

Even if you don't know the lineage of the piece, you have the ability to imagine it. And this is just as valid as knowing its provenance in terms of the meaning you assign to it when you're applying the Slow Style philosophy. I have an old shop sign in my home that says "Opera Hats/Don Hooton/International." I have no idea where this shop was located, and I don't know anything about the brands of hats that were sold there. But I can make

Right: Design by Zandra Zuraw; photo by Erin Little.

Opposite: Design by Sean Leffers; photo courtesy Elizabeth Carababas.

up my own story, which strengthens my bond with the sign and adds another layer of my own history to it, by the very fact that I have it hanging in my entryway.

My mother was trained as a classical ballet dancer and has devoted her life to the performing arts. One of the things she did for work was dance in the opera for those productions that required it. She performed in an old opera house with many of the grand, dramatic details we associate with the opera houses of Europe. And she loved it. She loved the formality and the way that going to the opera lifted people out of ordinary time and transported them to a place of refined artistic experience. As a little girl, I was thrilled to go backstage to the dressing rooms of that opera house. So when I

look at that sign hanging in my front entry, welcoming people to hang up their coats and hats, I imagine a time when people might have been hanging up their opera hats, as if I lived in a grand estate and was hosting the party of the year. It makes me smile every time.

How do we reconcile an antique piece in a home where the primary aesthetic is focused on the now, or the future? First, I would argue that the intentional use of one antique piece only serves to amplify all of the other modern pieces in a room. Look at what Sean Leffers did by juxtaposing this modern staircase with the antique vessels it curves around at the bottom. Together they make you think about the fact that each came from the mind of a human being, and how

Design by Anne Hulcher Tolletto of Hanover Avenue; photo by Helen Norman.

amazing the evolution of human creativity has been. It also speaks to the aesthetic of the person who lives there. Clearly, their interest in design doesn't fit into a single box. This room could so easily feel cold and sterile, but the patina of those large pots and the weave in the rattan chair warm everything up, giving the room a layered look that it wouldn't have otherwise.

Another important reason to incorporate antiques into every room is that it grounds the space and gives it a temporal context that would otherwise be missing in an all-contemporary room. That's because those very "of the moment" contemporary pieces you've just bought will start to show signs of their own time period very quickly. In a year or two, they'll start to feel dated. But when you anchor those pieces with an antique, suddenly you've expressed an awareness of the passage of time and the room feels intentionally put together, rather than just a combination of objects that simply reflect the 2024 Crate & Barrel catalog.

HOW TO MASTER THE MIX

In a Slow Styled home, it's really *all* about the mix. Not just old and new, but also different eras, different styles, different design elements. Why? Because mixing all of these things together is really the most honest way to represent the passage of time in our *own* lives. Rather than getting rid of something from an older phase of your life, try incorporating it with new (or new-to-you) things and see how they relate to one another. It's the inter-mingling of opposites that make a room really feel lived in and alive.

Design and photo by Natasha Habermann.

To really master the mix, pay attention to details. How does the piece connect to the rest of what's going on? You'll want to consider what elements are shared and what are opposed, across the furniture and objects you bring in. For example, in this beautiful entryway of Erica Swagler's home, she has an ornate settee with a formal frame hanging above it. To make sure people feel comfortable sitting there to take off their muddy shoes, she's added a simple block print pillow and a streamlined umbrella stand.

Design and photo by Erica Swagler.

Left and right: Design by Vestige Home; photos by Rebecca McAlpin.

I also love how Nicole Cole of Vestige Home has brought in some wood pieces to warm up these bathrooms full of smooth tile and porcelain. Do you have a bunch of smooth shiny things? Maybe you could look for some natural wood to warm things up.

Design by Vestige Home; photo by Rebecca McAlpin.

In another room by Nicole Cole, consider how the lines, shapes, and designs of antiques are used. This photo shows a luxurious marble fireplace from a time before our own. She topped it with a very large, antique carved mirror that further emphasized the grandeur of the room. But then, she lightened things up, with a mid-century chandelier that strikes the complete opposite in tone. It's the juxtaposition of the design elements that shows off your personality.

I think designer Anne Hulcher Tollett is particularly good at making sure a room doesn't take itself too seriously while still incorporating antiques. In the dining room, she uses a glass chandelier paired with Eames molded stacking chairs and a very modern painting that shakes up the all-neutral room with a dash of neon pink.

Design by Anne Tollett of Hanover Avenue; photo by Helen Norman.

If you already love antiques and can't pass by a thrift store without grabbing a shopping cart, everything I've said about being aware of how the piece will fit with the rest of the room applies here as well. To an untrained eye, all the things in this room may simply look "old." But Erica Swagler has actually mixed several different eras here, which gives the space a much more laid-back feel than it would if she had chosen items only from the era in which her home was built.

Aldous Bertram's vignettes are compilations of things he's found, bought, and created along the way. He literally wrote the book on the history of chinoiserie and often mixes together different motifs from that style, one of which is the foo dog. They're part of a larger collection he assembled over years of scouring antique markets. They stay relevant to his overall room designs because he takes his time, adds layers of things that delight him, and rearranges constantly. He's currently in a phase of collecting cloisonne birds!

If you really don't like contemporary design (that is, pieces made in the last twenty-five years), you can avoid the historic museum feeling by mixing together several definitive eras from the past. If you like antiques, you're probably also interested in the history of design, so do a little research into a few styles and take note of the materials used, the level of detail incorporated by the craftsmen, the scale of the furniture, and the visual weight each piece would take up in a room. Mixing together multiple design elements will keep the room feeling fresh, interesting, and created for how you actually live today.

Above Left: Design and photo by Erica Swagler.

Left: Design by Aldous Bertram; photo by Blake Shorter.

What I'm suggesting you try to do isn't necessarily easy or obvious. You may have to build up your confidence to make these bold combinations of styles and eras. You can start small. Buy a small antique piece such as a lamp or an antique tin to hold your kitchen utensils. See how that feels in the context of the rest of what you have. Live with it for a bit. And then let yourself be inspired to lean in toward more antiques or to go further toward the contemporary by allowing the antique piece to inform a new paint color that feels very modern.

In this eat-in kitchen designed by Natasha Habermann, she's mixing the humble origins of an old farmhouse table with a more ornate mantel. You can also see the Eames chairs and a contemporary light fixture. Tying it all together is an Oriental rug.

Photo by Natasha Habermann.

HOW TO SHOP FOR ANTIQUES AND VINTAGE ITEMS

If you're new to antiquing or thrifting, I'm excited to introduce you to the wonders you're about to discover! But I know you have questions. And maybe some concerns. If you have an aversion to poking around shelves crammed with dusty old things, I realize you've got some mental hurdles to overcome.

Large antique fairs, in particular, can be daunting for the sheer size of them. How are you supposed to know if something is worth the asking price, or if you're getting a deal? Not to mention, being inundated with so much eye candy, you might lose sight of what you actually need.

As I see it, there are two ways to shop for these treasures. One is to be open to whatever strikes your fancy. The other is to go with specific things in mind.

Design and photo by
Sean Leffers.

Shopping with Purpose

I almost never have a particular piece of furniture from a particular era and designer on my shopping list. For some people, especially very educated collectors, looking for something very specific is the thrill of the hunt. For me, the thrill comes more in the form of finding something that will solve a problem in a way I hadn't yet thought of. By "problem," I'm referring to the situations where I have a practical need—for storage, for privacy, to delineate an area in a room, and so on. So I start looking for furniture or accessories that will fit what I need.

If I'm looking for a side table, I'm not necessarily looking for a literal side table. I'm open to anything that has the right dimensions, surface, and materials. For example, when setting up our living room, I felt like there were an awful lot of legs (of furniture), crowding up the visual space along the bottom third of the room. As a solution, I took the long-legged side table out and replaced it with a stack of vintage suitcases. Different materials, no legs. Roughly the same dimension and height. It takes that part of the room from "fine" to "really interesting."

My advice here is to have the problem in mind, rather than the piece of furniture you think will solve it. Many different things can be used in multiple ways. China cabinets can be used to store kids' art supplies. Garden stools can be used as side tables. Stacks of books can be used to prop up a flat surface, creating a coffee table. I use an antique desk in our dining room to store linens.

Another way to shop with purpose is to think about a design element that may be missing from a room, such as the color black. I think a bit of black should

Opposite: Design by Zandra Zuraw; photo by Erin Little. Above: Design and photo by Natasha Habermann.

be in every room to ground things and to act as an exclamation point to some other dominant color. In this kitchen by Natasha Habermann, she has a palette that's mostly a mix of whites. The matte black faucet is an interesting foil, and bringing in a black metal lamp and a black wooden frame completes this corner. If you think your room could use a touch of black for the same reason, keep your mind open to a vase, a piece of art, a tray, or a picture frame as your eyes are scanning the antique shop. You can even squint a little as you're looking at the thrift store shelves and focus on the colors you see.

Narrowing things down by material is another way to go. In my living room, I needed more storage for books. I already had a wooden barrister bookcase, wooden crates used for other books, and a wooden coffee table. Because I had so much wood, I went looking for a cool metal bookcase (cool in terms of temperature) to offset the warm wood in the room. Eventually, I found old metal shelving for plants that had probably been outside for much of its life. Even better, instead of solid slabs of metal, the shelves were made up of a series of thin metal rods, giving the appearance of airiness. This made a nice foil to the heavy wood in the rest of the room.

Design by Zandra Zuraw; photo by Erin Little.

Embracing Serendipity

The second way to shop for antiques or vintage goods is to be completely open to whatever grabs your attention. In the overview to this book, I talked about serendipity as one of the main benefits of the Slow Style approach. It happens when you're simply poking around thrift and antique stores, hoping your eyes will alight on something unexpected and fantastic. I do this kind of shopping when I don't need anything in particular. I go because I might find inspiration in how a dealer has displayed their wares or how a shop owner has curated an experience. In addition to inspiration, I'm also always on the lookout for a gem that I didn't know I absolutely *had* to have.

Some of my favorite collections have started this way, purely out of joy. I find one slightly campy, silly, ceramic bird pitcher, and before you know it I've got three or four campy, silly, ceramic bird vessels that look amazing when displayed together.

Shopping for serendipity is when the real magic happens. It's when you find something that you never knew you wanted (much less, needed) and yet it becomes the focal point of the room, or the starting point for a whole makeover. It's the piece that elevates your room from generic to *wow*. While you're in the shop, picture where you would put the item that inspires you in your house. Imagine if it might strike up an interesting conversation. If you really like a picture,

Design by Zandra Zuraw; photo by Erin Little.

it comes home with you! Items I've acquired this way have always delighted my friends the most. They ask, "Where on earth did you get this?" I know that committing to something unexpected is what makes my home unique.

But how do you keep from getting overwhelmed? Start at a small shop, not a huge antique fair. Let your eyes slowly roam over all the objects you see and take a closer look at anything that catches your eye. Allow yourself to be drawn toward a shape, color, or material that you simply love. Often, I'll check out something because I have no idea what it is or what it was used for. Most antiques shops will have some kind of explanation on the tag, along with an estimated date, which is a great way to educate yourself.

Another idea is to be led by a favorite type of object (say, antique silver brushes that were part of a woman's bedtime routine), a particular maker (such as pottery by McCoy), or an iconic style, era, or time period. Aldous Betram's favorite century is the eighteenth century. He gravitates toward furniture and objects that resemble things he's seen in European country houses on his travels. And I've already mentioned his love of chinoiserie, a style that's lasted hundreds of years through numerous iterations. In this bedside vignette, you can see how it all comes together. For Aldous (and for many designers in this book, including myself), collecting is not a science or done according to a formula. He says, "I think everything goes together because it has been chosen with my eye, and therefore will naturally match

Design by Zandra Zuraw; photo by Erin Little.

Design by Aldous Bertram; photo by Blake Shorter.

with everything else." This continuous desire to move things around, play with shapes, colors, materials, eras, styles, makers, and so on really is the step-by-step way of mastering the mix.

The great thing about this kind of shopping is that it's really an exercise in developing your aesthetic point of view. As you're doing all of this looking, poking around, and contemplating objects that catch your eye, you're actually thinking about why you're drawn to one thing and not another, you're noticing what appeals to you, and you're logging information about patterns. What are you continually drawn to? Do you gravitate toward stripes, florals, animals, ceramics, painted wood, graphic lettering, pink, white, navy, orange? Maybe you've picked up Sean Scherer's newest book *Vignettes* and have studied his mastery. When he's creating a vignette, he often focuses simply on how

different shapes interact with each other. When you start purchasing a few things just because they give you a burst of happiness, you're in the process of developing your signature style.

Will you have regrets? Will you sometimes realize that the thing you thought you loved was really just a short-lived crush? Sure. But this is also part of figuring out who you are. When I'm antiquing with people and they pick up something that has clearly drawn them in, I hold my breath to see if they'll actually buy it. If it's not terribly expensive and they're taking a long time thinking about it, I know that they're dithering about how they'll use it, do they "need" it, where they'll put it, and whether or not it will "go" with things they already own. A huge sigh often comes next, and they put the treasure back down—and I'm thinking they've missed an opportunity.

Design and photo by Sean Scherer.

Now, I'm not saying you should buy everything that catches your eye or that you should never walk out of an antiques shop empty-handed. Nor am I saying that those questions running through the head of that person are invalid. I'm saying that eventually, if you want to create a home that means something, that represents who you are and who you're becoming, you're going to have to commit to a quirky object or two. It's the very act of assembling a group of items in a way that no one else has done that validates your expression of yourself as a one-of-a-kind individual.

Becoming a "junker" (as the beloved designer Mary Randolph Carter calls it) is always going to require a balance between restraint and madness. You might start out buying just one vintage tablecloth that you drape on your patio table to give the setting a little flair. And then you buy a couple more that you turn into pillowcases. And then curtains. Over time, you realize you now have a cache of vintage linens that you bought because you were *sure* you'd do something with them. It's been fifteen years and you realize you really don't want any more vintage linens in your decorating repertoire. That's when you sell them to people like me who are very happy you're ready to let them go.

Design by Carmen René Smith of Aquilo Interiors; photo by Meghan Caudill.

Design and photo by Sean Leffers.

All three of these woodblock prints are by Sabra Field. Design by Zandra Zuraw; photo by Erin Little.

ART

No house is a home without art

Those who have listened even occasionally to the Slow Style Home podcast can probably guess what I'm going to say in this chapter. Art is as essential to making a home as is a bed to sleep on, a chair to sit on, and a plate to eat from. You may flinch at that idea at first, but you're probably thinking of art with a capital "A." Art that you've seen in museums. Or art you've seen hanging in a historic home once decorated for a Getty or a Rockefeller.

I strongly believe that everyone deserves to have art in their lives because *everyone deserves to live with beauty.* Granted, it's not as essential as a solid roof and plumbing. But once the bare minimum of human rights is met, beauty is paramount. Why? Because the expression of beauty is what gives us our humanity.

People have had the instinct and drive to put their stamp on their surroundings forever. Think of the cave paintings at Lascaux, the statues buried with Egyptian kings, the stone carvings at Angkor Wat. The examples aren't all from royalty. Prisoners have learned to paint,

to make music, to write poetry . . . sometimes to save their souls and their sanity. And everywhere you go, no matter the level of poverty that's experienced, people adorn their lives with beauty in any way possible.

What's sad to me is the distance we've put between ourselves and the world of art in the last seventy-five years or so. We somehow became disentangled from the understanding that our predecessors had about the value of beauty and the creators who brought it forth. By the mid-twentieth century, we were so used to mass-produced things that mass-produced art just slipped right onto store shelves without much of a blink. The question of what to buy for our walls was answered not by what emotional experience we had while interacting with a painting, but by whether the painting had colors in it that matched our rugs and chairs. We no longer knew our own hearts well enough to trust that we knew what we loved when it came to choosing art.

Everything in her home is personal to artist Angela Chrusciaki Blehm, but nothing more so than her large collection of paintings and sculptures.

Photo by Angela Chrusciaki Blehm.

WHAT CONSTITUTES "ART"?

The answer to this question depends on who you ask. From the perspective of artists who have spent hours upon hours training their eyes and honing their technique, I can understand why they would differentiate "art" from just anything that someone happens to hang on the wall. I'm sympathetic to this because I've learned a lot about the skill, creativity, and imagination it takes to make a truly impressive piece of art. Perhaps your priority is to hang work that honors this kind of mastery. But if your priority is to live with things that give you great joy, then that opens up the possibilities of what you'll consider "art." These two goals can coexist, but it's good to make the distinction that what constitutes art is subjective.

I love seeing objects that don't belong in a frame hanging on the walls of a home. People have been elevating everyday items for a long time—showing off a silhouette, or a masterful work of joinery, or something with chipped paint and a different color poking through. It's a way of celebrating the life and work of someone who used their hands to accomplish things. So yes, hanging anything on the wall for the specific purpose of highlighting its aesthetic qualities rather than its *actual* purpose is worthy of taking up space.

This is where a lot of people start. Your great-grandmother's wooden spoons, a collection of old wire rug beaters, farm implements, you name it . . . all of these things have interesting shapes and back stories. And, maybe most enticing to the person who hasn't learned much about art up to this point, they are affordable.

Erica Swagler has hung a collection of antique mirrors along the wall, the frames of which add an interesting geometry to the space. An added benefit is how they bounce light all around the stairwell.

Photo by Erica Swagler.

Design and photo by
Sean Leffers.

Once you start hanging these kinds of objects on your walls and living with them for a while, you start understanding on a visceral level what a huge difference art makes to the overall feeling of your home. Presumably, what you choose to hang—be it tools, cookware, baskets, love letters—you're choosing because you have some kind of personal connection to it. In this way, you start to see how your story is reflected back at you and your home becomes as unique as you are.

What *doesn't* count as art? I can't say that mass-produced art you buy at Home Goods isn't "art." Obviously, it's *meant* to be art. What I can say is that mass-produced

This large giclée print by Treacy Ziegler was one of the first pieces we bought.

Photo by Erin Little.

art doesn't do the job of one-of-a-kind art where you can see the imprint of the artist in the object itself. But even that's a questionable definition. There are painters who do limited runs using a giclée printing technique. And there are woodblock artists who also do limited runs. Photographers have been printing multiples of their work for decades, and there are sculptors who create the same piece using a mold that they've made so that more than one person can have their sculpture. These are all more affordable ways for people to purchase art while still giving the artist a fair compensation. So it's not nec- essarily the "one-of-a-kind" factor that qualifies something as "real" art. You could even

Rydhima Brar has hung a vintage movie poster that sets the tone for the entire living area.

Photo by Pablo Enriquez.

argue that at some point in the product development and manufacturing process, someone actually painted something before it was mass-produced. (Until mass production starts using AI, of course, but that is another discussion.)

The difference then, between what I'm encouraging you to hang on your walls and what you can find at big-box stores, is an emotional connection between you and the piece. And that's really hard to have with something that's mass-produced simply because those things have been stripped of their humanity. I'd rather see sheets torn from a *National Geographic* magazine (which is, of course, mass-produced) than mass-produced art hung on the walls because it tells the story of *you* searching through magazines, making a choice of which photos hit you viscerally enough to

bother hanging them. Posters of your favorite movies, concerts, or travel destinations can also play a part in your personal narrative and are less expensive.

Yes, art is what you make of it. And you get to choose what it is you call "art." What I'm suggesting is that you take your time choosing what's going to go on your walls so that your choices reflect some deeper aspect of who you are, the humor you find in life, or the aspirations you have going forward. That's the true job art has in our homes. Sometimes that comes from what you choose to hang. Sometimes it comes from how you hang it. Sometimes it comes from what you pair it with. As long as there's a thoughtful (or thought-provoking) intention behind it, the art you choose will be part of defining your own personal style.

This is one of Angela Chrusciaki Blehm's own pieces above the couch. It fully reflects Angela's femininity, confidence, and wild sense of humor.

Photo by Angela Chrusciaki Blehm.

THE EVOLUTION OF AN ART COLLECTOR

In sharing the last twenty-five years of my own passage—from hanging posters to selecting one-of-a-kind pieces from artists I discovered in galleries—I hope you'll see how you, too, can become a collector. My love of art came early with a board game called Masterpiece. I played this with my dad, and we would compete to see who could remember the most about a famous painting depicted on the front of the game cards, with the answers on the back. I was weirdly good at memorizing these things and it still helps me watching *Jeopardy* today.

In college I took an art history course on a whim, and I truly fell in love. It was Northern Renaissance Art, and the teacher showed us that there were symbols hidden within the paintings, some in plain sight. Each one was a mystery to be solved, and I was hooked. My college was close to New York City, and I began going to the museums, seeing colors and shapes and materials as if I had never come across these things before.

My development as an art fanatic started with posters of artwork I found in museum gift shops. It turns out, the poster phase is a pretty common entryway into becoming a collector of one-of-kind art. About college age, you choose the posters that reflect your passions and beliefs so that you begin to

Design by Zandra Zuraw; photo by Erin Little.

distinguish yourself from your roommates, claiming your individuality.

Over the years, I've collected several different kinds of art at thrift stores. Seeing something that fits into my collection, framed and hanging askew amongst lots of other eye candy is still thrilling. My gateway drug was vintage paint-by-numbers. The first one I found appealed to me because of the color palette and the paint itself, which you could tell was from a different time. I also loved the cheekiness of paint-by-numbers and the quaintness of that pastime that was popular when I was very young.

Your next step might be your first purchase of an amateur painting at an antiques store. Or maybe, you first purchase directly from an artist at an art fair. You're still highly aware of price, either because you don't have a lot of money, or you're unaware of how to gauge the value of what you think of as "real" art. I bought this little oil painting from a street artist named Miguel López Mora on a trip to Madrid. Not only do I love the colors, I love the idea of celebrating something as humble as an egg.

Eventually, all of the above led me into collecting nautical subjects in both paint-by-numbers and one-of-a-kind oils, though the oils were still inexpensive, presumably because they were done by unknown student artists. This collection came about because of the strong ties my family has to nautical subjects from living near the sea. Today, you can see my thrifting scores in our stairwell where there's an ode to the ocean hung in a dramatic diagonal line. I've combined paint-by-numbers and oils along with the front of an old crate, the cover of a paperback book, and a selection of fishing lures. This is a good example of turning objects into art, simply by hanging them on a wall and displaying them with art that deliberately came from a brush, paints, and canvas.

My powder room is where you'll see another mix of materials: paint-by-numbers, thrifted oils, memorabilia, and hand-me-downs from my grandfather, all related to my love of travel. I started this bathroom redo during the pandemic when travel was out of the question, and I keep adding to it. I dug out a vintage airline ticket I had picked up years earlier. I'm always drawn to vintage travel items, in part because my dad was a travel agent back when travel still had an aura of glamor around it. I framed the old ticket, boarding pass, and baggage claim tags, complete with the itinerary of someone going to Zurich, Paris, and Rome (sigh!). You'll also see a current paint-by-number that depicts myself and a dear friend in Madrid. She found a company that turned her photo of us into a paint-by-number kit, complete with

Design by Zandra Zuraw; photo by Erin Little.

Painting by Ruth Scotch; design by Zandra Zuraw; photo by Erin Little.

corresponding numbered paint containers. It was such a lovely gift and so meditative to complete!

The more I educated myself in the art of decorating, the more I appreciated the compositions created by masters of the still-life genre. And so began another collection in my office, which doubles as a guest room. I now make a beeline for any still life that catches my attention in antique stores, knowing I still have a few spaces left on my walls. Collecting these paintings was the last little push I needed to sign up for an art class. I'd wanted to do this forever but had never made the time. After seeing and collecting so many paintings at different skill levels (sometimes the amateur paintings are my favorites), I finally committed to a week-long course, taught by my friend, Ruth Scotch, who is both a wonderful teacher and a professional artist. We own two of her paintings. One

is a portrait of our boys when they were young, and the other we bought simply because we loved the composition, the colors, and the brushstrokes.

My husband shares my passion for art but he's not as entranced by amateur work as I am. So the rest of our home is dedicated to art that's done by people who we feel have achieved a certain level of mastery. All of this artwork we found together. Early in our marriage, my husband and I started buying original pieces of art while on vacation. These were things we happened upon, were drawn to, and didn't seem all that expensive to us. We didn't really have anything to measure price by, so we just did what felt right.

A few years into our marriage, we planned our first vacation with the primary purpose of learning about and buying art. Good friends of ours who had been collecting for a long time pointed us toward Santa Fe, New Mexico, a city that supports one of the largest art markets in the United States. There are more galleries there than you'll have time to see, representing artists of every medium, style, and subject matter. There is also a great variety of price points. Each gallery is run by a helpful and passionate gallerist. When I saw this painting by Amy Donaldson, my first thought was "I want to wake up to this every morning." In my mind, that's as good a reason as any to buy a piece of art! It turns out it didn't hang as beautifully in the bedroom as it does here in the dining room. But I still feel the same way.

We packed up our three-month-old son, changed diapers in the trunk of the rental car, and used rolled-up blankets in a dresser drawer as a makeshift crib. We spent all of our extra money on art. (By the way, three-month-olds turn out to be the perfect age for this kind of trip. They're too young to walk, they easily sleep in a stroller, and they get lots of adoring attention from everyone.) While we were in Santa Fe, we went headlong into the process of educating ourselves on artistic skill and creativity, as well as beginning to understand how to evaluate a painting's worth to us. We've now gone to Santa Fe a total of four times, and we'll go many more in the future.

At this point, most of our walls are full and we even have a couple of pieces that we rotate in and out, depending on the amount of room we have to work with when we buy something new. We've also increased our spending budget as our understanding of the value of artwork has developed. To us, it's not strange to see a painting by a working artist cost as much, or more than, what most would consider an expensive, high-end piece of furniture. We'd been following this artist, Sandra Pratt, for several years before finally committing to one of her paintings. The process of following her work and staying in touch with the gallery is part of the story in terms of our feelings toward the piece.

Painting by Amy Donaldson from Gaia Contemporary; design by Zandra Zuraw; photo by Erin Little.

HOW TO START AN ART COLLECTION

I hope it's clear from my personal story that you don't need to wait until you're filthy rich to collect art, you don't need to geek out on art history (unless you want to), and you'll probably start your collection without even realizing it. It only takes a few things on the wall that you fall deep and hard for, and you're on your way.

To actively start collecting, I recommend first and foremost that you look at a lot of art. This is not just to educate yourself on different aspects of the history and techniques of creating art, but rather simply to know what you love. Luckily, it's pretty easy to expose yourself to lots of art these days. In person, you have museums, of course, but you also have galleries, open studio tours, "First Friday" events, coffee shops, and local arts and crafts shows. Besides going out and seeing art in real life, you have Instagram. There may be other great places online to see art, but my favorite social media platform for discovery is Instagram.

When you're looking at art, go just for fun. Make note of what you're drawn to. Is it portraits? Abstracts? Seascapes? Fiber arts? What colors do you love? What subject matter pulls you in? How do you feel about paintings, photography, sculpture, and mixed media? There are no rules. You get to decide what *you* like. Once you see patterns in what you're drawn to, I recommend learning a bit more about those pieces: how they're made, who made them, and so on. You may find you love certain pieces even more.

Opposite: Painting by Sandra Pratt, Giacobbe-Fritz Fine Art gallery, Santa Fe; design by Zandra Zuraw; photo by Erin Little.

Above: Design and photo by Angela Chrusciaki Blehm.

By now you know I strongly believe that having art, of some kind . . . any kind . . . is crucial to creating a beautiful, meaningful home. So how do you choose? Start with something you feel you can afford, and make sure you love, love, love it. You might love it for its subject matter, or a personal connection you have to it. You might love it simply for the colors or materials it's made of. As long as it stops you in your tracks or you feel a flutter in your stomach. Still not sure if it's the right piece for you? Here are some questions to ask yourself:

- Can I imagine walking out of here without this piece and never thinking about it again?

- How would I feel if I came back next month and saw that it was gone?

- Do I want to wake up each day and have that be the first thing I see?

- If I were to sit in my favorite spot in the house, is this what I'd want to be staring at?

Vignette with vintage oil painting and objects artfully arranged by Sean Scherer.

Photo by Sean Scherer.

A short kimono, which is an early nineteenth-century Japanese boro piece from antiques dealer David Alan in Solana Beach, hangs in Sean Leffers' home.

Photo by Sean Leffers.

Artwork and photo by Angela Chrusciaki Blehm.

Above: Design and photo by Angela Chrusciaki Blehm.

Opposite: Art by Barbara Bowles; design by Zandra Zuraw; photo by Erin Little.

Once you have your first piece, or a few pieces, you'll come up against a decision about whether you're going to start a collection (based on subject matter, style, and so on) or if you're going to add something that's completely different from what you've already bought.

I've done both. With the less expensive things, I feel they have more impact as part of a collection, while the more exceptional pieces seem to want to stand on their own. I'm not necessarily expecting my paint-by-numbers and amateur oils to remain of interest to me for decades (although they may). They're delighting me because they're part of a group, expressing my interests as of right now.

When it comes to pieces I've invested in with my husband, we are looking at them with a more critical eye, doing some research on the artists' processes, learning about the techniques they're using, and thinking about how they relate to our other pieces of art. More serious art collectors (and ones with much bigger budgets) might want to collect as much as they can from one particular artist or things that represent a particular school of art, coming from a specific place and time. Because we're interested in all kinds of different mediums, and we want to continue to be surprised by new forms and interpretations, we've decided to go more broadly. So far, we have a mix of collage, woodblock, photography, oil, acrylic, giclée, and sculptures made of wood and bronze. Hanging in our bedroom is a photograph of my favorite kind of vintage truck, weathered over the years with multiple layers of paint chipping away. Because it's a close-up, it's more of an abstract piece than just a literal photo of a truck.

It's a good idea to stretch yourself, even at the beginning, in terms of how much money to spend. I don't mean spending above your means. I mean spending more than you might for something that's utilitarian because you believe the piece is worth it *to you*. Of course, sometimes you come across a new artist and they're selling their work for less than they really need to. Perhaps they're still unsure of themselves or

Painting above fireplace by Ron Johnson; design by Anne Hulcher Tollett of Hanover Avenue; photo by Helen Norman.

they are hoping to get their work out there by making it more affordable. Here are some final questions to ask yourself when trying to decided whether or not to buy a piece:

- Do I know where I'm going to hang it?

- Can I think of at least one alternative place to hang it if the first spot doesn't work?

- Is it too big, too small, or just the right size for the spot I'm thinking of?

- If it's too small, do I have something else I can hang with it, even temporarily?

- How many cafe lattes, dinners out, or other

indulgences would I have to give up to afford this?

- If it's much more expensive than other pieces roughly the same size, do I understand why it's priced so much higher?

- If it's much less expensive than other pieces roughly the same size, do I feel like I'd be compromising quality for price?

These aren't trick questions. There are no right or wrong answers that I'm trying to lead you toward. Because art is subjective, it's hard to know if you should buy something based on quantitative measures. These are just gut-check questions to help you make decisions while considering things like practicality, cost, and value.

HOW TO BRAVE THE GALLERY SCENE

Here are a few things to know if you're unsure about going to galleries:

You belong there. Don't let *anyone* make you feel as if you're not smart enough, rich enough, or "hip" enough to go to a gallery. All kinds of people love and buy art. No one is going to ask you to leave. Which brings me to the next point.

The piece above the bed is one of Angela Chrusciaki Blehm's own.

Photo by Angela Chrusciaki Blehm.

The gallerists might ignore you. If they *are* under the *mistaken* impression that you don't belong there, they may simply leave you alone. This can be a good thing. Taking your time walking around the gallery, stopping when something catches your eye, talking with the other person you came with about what you're loving and what you're hating . . . this is all part of the gallery experience. I've only felt out of place once—and it wasn't a gallery, it was a shop in Venice that sold very, very expensive fabrics. In that case, I didn't stay long because the shop owner was standing very close to me, following me around, making me uncomfortable. If this happens, you can leave and cross that gallery off your list. But it's very uncommon.

Gallerists aren't expecting you to make a purchase just because you walked into their space. If you're worried about pushy salespeople, you likely won't find them here. They know that what they're selling aren't impulse purchases. They expect you to take your time, and frequently to come back a few times before buying anything. In one case, it took us three visits over the course of two separate vacations to buy just one piece by an artist my husband and I had been following. If the gallery is run by the artist themself, it can feel a little trickier. Just be polite, ask questions if you have them, but always know it's perfectly fine to walk away without buying anything.

Galleries often have open studio events, which can be a nice place to start. Many places will designate a few days each year to make an event out of walking the town and visiting the studios of working artists. And a lot of galleries take part in "First Friday" events, which can actually happen on any day of the week. This is when a group of galleries open their doors in the evenings, offer wine and cheese, and encourage people to come all at once and see what's new. What's great about these designated event days is that you'll be there with lots of other people, so if you're nervous about being all alone in a gallery and feeling out of place, this is a good way to get your feet wet.

You need to see a lot of art. You need to see how different artists interpret the same subjects. You need to see the different techniques people use to create their art. Sometimes it's helpful to overhear different reactions to a piece that has caught the attention of several people. You can do this in museums, of course, but galleries offer up-close and personal experiences with up-and-coming artists and working artists in a way that museums can't. It's more intimate and potentially more educational. Gallery visits will also help develop your sense of what things cost and how the prices align with how much you value what you're seeing.

Opposite: Painting by Sarah Boyts Yoder; living area designed by Anne Hulcher Tollett of Hanover Avenue; photo by Helen Norman.

A mix of thrift store and gallery pieces on display by Katie Saro.

Photo by Katie Saro.

HOW TO HANG ART

The following suggestions are all things to take into consideration, depending on the situation. There are ways in which art is typically hung, but there are times when you have to think a little differently.

The Rule: Don't hang art too high.

Most art looks best when it's hung at eye level. I realize that eye level for a five-foot-four person is different than eye level for a six-foot-two person. If you live in a home with this kind of discrepancy between people, shoot for somewhere in between. Keeping the art at a human scale grounds it within the space and draws you in, allowing the best emotional connection between art and viewer.

Design by Sean Leffers. Photograph above the window: a portrait of Yukio Mishima by Eikoh Hosoe from their collaborative photobook, *Killed by Roses*. The painting on the left is by an unknown artist that Sean bought in Marché Aux Puces Saint Ouen (possibly the world's most sought-after "flea" market, found in Paris. On the back is written "mon fils," presumably meaning that this artist was doing a portrait of his or her son.

Photo of living area courtesy Elizabeth Carababas.

Design and photo by
Sean Scherer.

When to break this rule: Sean Leffers has hung a photograph high above a window. Your eyes are drawn upward, away from the rest of the room. Hanging it in this way heightens the drama of the image.

Do this instead: Hang the piece in relation to what's around it, rather than centering it on the wall. The artwork should feel as if it's part of a conversation with the furniture, not left out on its own. This is especially true when you have a small piece of art on a large wall. Rather than drawing attention to how small the artwork is, hang it lower and closer to the top of the furniture, as Sean Scherer has done with these two small pieces hung close to the chair. When you do this, you're carving out moments in your home, dotted around a room, and using the artwork as part of a larger composition that includes furniture and accessories.

The Rule: The size of the piece should make sense with the size and shape of the wall.

In other words, you don't usually want a dinky little painting on a great big wall, or a painting that's the wrong orientation for the wall. This painting fits perfectly here, and Rydhima Brar has it just leaning against the wall, rather than hung, which is always an option.

Left: Design by Rydhima Brar of R/terior Studio; photo by Eric Lucero.

Opposite: Design by Vestige Home, photo by Brian Wetzel.

Above: Design by Carmen René of Aquilo Home; photo by Meghan Caudill.

When to break this rule: In the photo on page 150, you see a large entryway. To fill the space, designer Nicole Cole is working with a small bench and a collection of small pieces of art. If she were to hang the artwork centered above the bench, it would collapse the energy of the room into the center. By taking the frames and putting them off to the right in a slight diagonal, she creates energy in the space by directing the eye upward. Using a dynamic, patterned wallpaper creates an intentional composition.

Do this instead: This is where a fabulous gallery wall comes in. There are many great examples out there but this one by Carmen René Smith is one of my favorites.

And lastly, *If you're scared of making holes in the wall, don't be.* Seriously, it's just not that big of a deal to leave behind a tiny little hole. And if it bothers you, spackling that hole and painting over it is so easy! If, however, you really have an aversion to moving things around your walls and making lots of holes, try this: lay your painting or object on top of some paper you've laid out on the floor. (Tape some newspaper pages together until it's bigger than the piece.) Trace around the painting or object and then cut out the shape to make a template. Hang the template with painter's tape (which is removable) and stand back to test out where you've hung it. This can be especially helpful when you're putting together a gallery wall.

MORE INSPIRATION

In addition to the previous rules of thumb, here are some ideas to shake loose any preconceived ideas you have about what you can and can't do with art.

- *Think beyond the living and dining rooms.* Hanging art in places that feel more utilitarian, such as a laundry room, kitchen, or bathroom, makes that room feel like it's part of the entire home. Side note: In wet, humid spaces, you probably won't want to hang something that is too precious. There are ways to mount paintings and photographs that offer some (but not total) protection. Other materials may stand up better to those environments, or simply hang your thrift store art that you're not too worried about in those spaces.

- *Use color effectively.* Art doesn't have to hang on white walls to look good. I've got nothing against white walls, and they are a no-fail choice if your primary purpose in the room is to focus on the artwork. But if your favorite color is, say, blush pink, don't be afraid to use it! I'm not sure which came first in this room by Natasha Habermann. Did she choose the wall color and then look for a painting that would be fantastic on top? Or was she inspired to choose that wall color from the pink in the painting? Either way, you get a sense of who this person is by the color in both.

- *Purposefully hang things off center.* You'd expect the formal mirror to be centered over the formal fireplace. Instead, Nicole Cole hung it off-center, playing with asymmetry, making everything feel more relaxed and allowing room for something natural and organic to be changed out regularly.

Design and photo by Katie Saro.

Painting by Grace B. Keogh; design and photo by Natasha Habermann.

Design by Vestige Home; photo by Rebecca McAlpin.

Rearrange your artwork regularly. The great thing about acquiring new art is that you may be forced to move things around to make room for the new piece. I love this because the room gets a burst of energy when you change things up, and I get a dopamine hit from seeing an "old" piece in a new way. Even if you haven't acquired something new recently, you can still get those benefits by rotating your art. It's literally the cheapest way to make over the entire feel of a space.

I hope I've now convinced you of a few things. One, you really do need to have art in your home. Two, it needs to be meaningful to you. Three, you have no reason to be intimidated by art galleries. You belong there. You deserve beauty in your life. And finally, collecting art is *fun*.

NATURE

Bringing nature into our interiors is essential

T he built environment" is an academic term also used in the architecture industry that does a great job of describing what the profession is about. It points to the fact that what is man-made is static ("built") and always situated within what is natural ("environment"). Our homes and the environments in which they are built, are inextricably linked.

Taking into consideration your environment and the natural world is part of the design process when creating your Slow Styled home. Maybe you live in a remote spot that winds through a forest to get to a shimmering lake, where you are surrounded by nature. Or maybe you live in a big city with lots of concrete, pavement, steel, glass, and brick. But even in a city there is still the air, sky, parks full of trees, grass, plants, and even little weeds pushing up through the sidewalk that will inform your design choices in terms of connecting to nature. In this chapter, I'll talk about the many aesthetic cues (such as color, shape, and texture) we can take from what surrounds us to help us create a beautiful, meaningful home.

Design by Vestige Home; photo by Brian Wetzel.

TAKING AESTHETIC CUES FROM NATURE

Bringing in natural elements and dotting them throughout your home is one of the easiest ways to create a dynamic interior. Yet a plant, fallen branch, or seashell do more than add to our decor. They can also teach you design principles if you take a closer look.

Color

Whenever you're not sure if two or more colors "go" together, look for an Instagram account that's dedicated to birds and start scrolling. Members of the Slow Style Society (check it out at slowstylehome. com/society-sales-page) might be rolling their eyes when they read this because I've used the bird analogy *many* times in my coaching with them! Looking at how mother nature has composed the huge variety of colors (not to mention patterns) in birds' feathers will show you right away that pretty much anything "goes" together. There are single birds with ten different colors on their bodies and they look just grand to me! Really pay attention to all of the different shades in the feathers, how much of each color is represented, which colors are next to each other, and which are separated by a neutral white or black. Just for fun, pull up a photo of a bird that you think is absolutely beautiful and create a mood board. Choose one color for the bed, one for the rug, and one for lamps, walls, and window treatments. I promise this is a no-fail approach to choosing color.

Opposite: Design by Vestige Home; photo by Brian Wetzel.

Left: Design Rydhima Brar of R/terior Studio; photo by Pablo Enriquez.

Nature offers color inspiration in so many forms. Currently, my den's color palette and pattern come from several photos of the northern New Mexico landscape. Any images of landscapes you have, especially ones that are very personal to you from a favorite spot, are a great place to start when choosing colors. What's important is that you pay attention to the nuances you see in the colors. How saturated or washed-out are they? How much of each color is showing up in the overall composition? What is the natural light like in the photo and how are the shadows playing a part in the mood? Once you start paying attention to these details it will help you replicate that in your color choices. You'll be using these colors not just on the walls, but in your fabrics, too, which means you can play with the materiality to accomplish the look you're going for.

Design by Zandra Zuraw; photo by Erin Little.

Shape

Nature also teaches us a lot about shape. There are very few right angles in nature. Most everything has curves, twists, and bends, like branches going off in wonky directions. Think of the veining in marble, the patterns in bark, or the perfectly curved spiral of the nautilus shell. Rydhima Brar's bedroom vignette has plenty of texture going on in the shag carpet, velvet bedspread, and fluted dresser. The two leaves from a monstera plant add a wonderful organic shape in contrast to all the straight lines.

Design and photo by
Natasha Habermann.

If you're struggling to figure out why your room lacks energy or feels lifeless, see if you have any natural items in the room. Nature adds organic shapes to our rooms that are unpredictable and, if it's a living plant, constantly changing. The curved, angular, and irregular lines of natural items give visual movement to the space and let us know that a real human lives there.

Play around with the direction of the arc formed by a tulip or shell or branch or antler. Try it where the arc is curved inward toward other objects, and then curved away. See which way you like best. There's no right or wrong, but there are specific things to make note of. Objects arcing toward something else tend to frame the space, focusing on whatever the end of the arc is pointing to. If the natural element is arching away from other things, it tends to open up the space. Organic shapes keep the eye moving, taking us up, down, over, and around our spaces. We need both—places for our eyes to rest and places for our eyes to travel.

Design by Aldous Bertram; photo by Blake Shorter.

Texture

In addition to learning from the shapes seen in nature, also consider the textures. Look at the living room photo by designer Rydhima Brar. The wood in the coffee table offers a raw, natural, organic foil to the sleek, smooth feel of the rest of the room. And in the kitchen by Nicole Cole (page 132), adding a lightweight branch of delicate greenery is a respite from the heaviness of the stove and counters.

When you look at the architectural bones of this office by Anne Hulcher Tollett (page 132), you might be tempted to lean toward a formal tone to elicit the feeling of getting some serious work accomplished. Instead, Anne lightens the mood by adding hits of natural texture. The bamboo shades, the heavy cotton curtains (with the added benefit of a folk-style floral motif), the jute rug, even the colorful porcelain elephant, allow the person at the desk to relax a little bit so that creative thinking can take place.

Design by Rydhima Brar of R/terior Studio; photo by Frank Francis.

Design by Vestige Home; photo by Rebecca McAlpin.

Design by Anne Hulcher Tollett of Hanover Avenue; photo by Helen Norman.

CHOOSING NATURAL ELEMENTS

I'm a big fan of using natural elements in our homes beyond the now-ubiquitous house-plant. Oh, I love houseplants and we'll get to them in a minute. Just don't overlook how useful *anything* from nature can be when composing a room or styling a vignette.

What's driven my own choice of natural elements is my love of curiosity cabinets from Great Britain's Victorian era. Wealthy people took extended voyages into lands foreign to them (or paid someone to do it), and came home with plant, animal, and mineral

My husband's grandfather made this box to store his nails and screws. It makes a wonderful display case for my bits of odds and ends. It holds things like shells I've picked up on the beach, vintage matchbooks featuring old seafood restaurants, and a few small animals made of papier-mâché, wood, and silver.

Photo by Erin Little.

Photo by Erin Little.

specimens that were unusual or foreign to the English natural world. Cabinets were created to display these wonders, piquing the curiosity and envy of friends.

Despite the colonial undertones of this practice, I love imagining what it was like for the first people in any culture to come across the skull of an animal never seen in their native lands. Or what it was like to be shown indigo dye or turmeric spice for the first time. It must have been as thrilling for them as it is for a child to play in their first snowfall. That's the draw of curiosity cabinets for me, to take the time to examine and appreciate the intricate, surprising beauty of the natural world.

My own curiosity has led me to collect shells, antlers (shed naturally), bones, and skulls of creatures found in the forest. I also collect feathers and, most recently, when we were traveling in Cambodia, a box covered in stingray skin (shagreen, which is the "leather" that comes from shark and ray skin).

I know this isn't for everyone. Some people don't want any animal remnants in their homes, and I certainly don't condone black markets for things such as rhino horns or elephant tusks. What I'm suggesting here is, as with any decor choice, you make it because you have an emotional reaction to or a personal experience with your choice.

Think about what parts of nature you are most in love with. If you love hiking in the woods, pick up something that's fallen on the trail. Nothing could be simpler than placing a few leaves or rocks on a windowsill or mantel, and yet look how dynamic and energetic this branch is in the vignette by Natasha Habermann. When you start bringing in these treasures, you're allowing the natural world to find its place in the rhythm of your home.

Design and photo by Natasha Habermann.

NATURE'S MOTIFS

Our love affair with the natural world seems innate. Humans have been capturing nature's beauty in art and objects for millennia. Today, references show up in clothing, food packaging, logos, book covers, stationery, and more. Once you start thinking about natural elements and organic shapes, you'll start seeing them everywhere. If you want to bring nature into your home beyond caring for a plant or two, you can use natural motifs in your curtains, pillows, tablecloths, and wallpaper, as well as motifs painted on or carved in wood, stone, or metal.

Erica Swagler has a soft, cottage rose pattern on her sofa that contrasts nicely with a branch of spiky, ethereal Japanese maple on her mantel. You also can look beyond plants when finding ways to mimic nature. Think of the drama when you break open a rock to reveal crystals inside. This chandelier in a dining room by Beth Diana Smith is reminiscent of bladed crystal habits such as kyanite or vivianite.

Designer and artist Aldous Bertram's love for chinoiserie is evident when you look throughout his home and see its influence everywhere. There is lots of bamboo and everything from coral and shells to monkeys and birds to orchids and pineapples. His home is fanciful, delightful, and full of nature-inspired motifs that have interested him for a long time. What keeps his rooms from looking overly thematic is how he mixes it all together. He uses antique pieces of chinoiserie paired with modern takes on those designs and the combination often adds a bit of humor dotted around his home.

Opposite: Design and photo by Beth Diana Smith.

Above Left: Design and photo by Erica Swagler.

Above Right: Design by Aldous Bertram; photo by Blake Shorter.

Design by Aldous
Bertram; photo by
Blake Shorter.

LIVING THINGS

Let's talk about houseplants. I love that they've come back into vogue. I grew up in the '70s when spider plants in macramé hangers were all the rage. Then, in the neon and plastic world of the '80s, they kind of disappeared. Now that houseplants are back in style, I hope they're here to stay because they give us several valuable things. One, it's good for our mental health to care for any other living thing. Two, they're good for our physical health because they purify our indoor air. And three, they make terrific accessories. "Stick a plant on it" sums up some of my best decorating advice! (Not really, but . . . well, kind of.)

This is probably a good time to bring up faux plants and flowers. I won't judge you for having them. I just won't like them. I don't care how good the faux is, I can tell. I can't put my finger on why I don't care for them. My knee-jerk reaction is to say, "What's the point in having something that's trying so hard to look real when you know it's not?" I understand some of the reasons I've heard for going with faux instead of real. Some people say they always kill whatever they try to grow, or they don't have the bandwidth to learn how to care for plants. Some people travel all the time and can't take care of living things. One of our members in the Slow Style Society has a cat whose mission in life is to knock over every single thing placed on every single surface.

I'm not judging the reasons you've chosen to go faux. I just think that sticking with dried plants, other natural materials (like shells or branches), floral patterns, and accessories such as lamps or rugs with natural motifs is a more authentic way of bringing nature into your home. It's also one less way to be living with plastic. And as for that brown thumb, there are a few plants that are truly hard to kill, especially if you don't have a ton of sunlight in your home. I've had good luck with spider plants, ZZ plants, snake plants, and pothos. Maybe you can turn your brown thumb green if you give some of these a try.

Here are a few examples of bringing nature in that don't require a green thumb. Below Left: Erica Swagler is using the organic shape of dried hydrangeas to give this area visual movement. Below Right: Beth Diana Smith chose to wallpaper the ceiling in a flora and fauna wallpaper, from which she's hung a chandelier reminiscent of a lotus flower. Opposite: Sean Scherer has hung an art deco sunburst mirror in his home.

Design and photo by Erica Swagler.

Design and photo by Beth Diana Smith.

Design and photo by Sean Scherer.

CARING FOR HOUSEPLANTS

I'm a much better outdoor gardener than I am an indoor plant parent. The main difference, as I see it, is that you have so much more responsibility for how the soil is maintained when your plant is in a pot rather than in the ground. I'll say upfront that there are many places besides this book where you should get advice about caring for houseplants. In fact, I've listed my favorites in the Resources section at the back of this book. So here, I'm just going to share what I've learned from my own trial and error when it comes to keeping plants alive indoors.

First, light really matters. If the instructions say "part sun," that does *not* mean that the plant will survive in a north-facing window that only gets indirect light for a few hours a day. I can't tell you how many poor plants I've killed because I was using all my wishing power that "part sun" was another way of saying "mostly shade." If you are blessed with lots of sunny windows, I'm jealous. You have a greater range of plants to choose from. If you don't, really stick with the ones that do well in low light. You can even buy plants online if you can't find them in the garden centers near you.

The second thing I've learned the hard way is not to overwater. I know it feels like you're not being attentive if you don't water every day, but for most of my plants, I was drowning them. And forget containers without drainage holes! That's practically a *guarantee* that your plant will die. I don't care how cute the pot is, if it doesn't have a drainage hole it won't support life, so forget it—or, if you must, put the plant in a proper pot that goes *inside* the pretty pot. I now err on the side of underwatering and my plants have lasted a lot longer. I generally water once every seven to ten days. If the soil is particularly dry, and the leaves are drooping, I'll give the plant a boost of extra hydration. And don't worry … droopy leaves almost always perk up after a good watering. But once a plant has drowned, there's no coming back.

The last thing I've experimented with is fertilizing the soil. I don't like to let a plant stay in the plastic pot it came in for more than six months. I let it acclimate to my home for a little while and then, when I start to notice the soil doesn't look rich and loamy, I'll repot. Repotting is a good time to fertilize because you can get those nutrients down into the lower layers of soil. Otherwise, you'll use fertilizers from the top down, which don't work as well (although they certainly don't hurt).

Opposite: Katie Saro has plenty of light for her fiddle-leaf fig between these windows.

Photo by Katie Saro.

Design and photo by Sean Leffers.

STYLING WITH PLANTS

There are many ways in which you can use houseplants as part of your aesthetic. Plants come in all different shapes, sizes, and densities. When I've got a tall, skinny area to fill, I'll add a snake plant. Their spiky leaves stand up straight to the sky and the plants don't get very wide. When I need to fill a wide space, I can use a bushy plant or a large leafed one, as Rydhima Brar did on this staircase.

If you've got a lot of hard surfaces, then something with leaves that has a lacy, airy quality would break up the density of it all, as you see here in Natasha Habermann's kitchen.

Choose pots thoughtfully. They can make a statement, blend in with your surroundings, or add to a feeling of clutter, depending on what you choose. I think the easiest way to avoid a cluttered look is to buy all terra-cotta pots. First, they almost always have holes in the bottom, and you already know how I feel about drainage holes. Second, they're inexpensive and come in all kinds of shapes and sizes. Third, they're made of such a classic, natural material they tend to work when paired with any other style.

Generally speaking, you can achieve a cohesive look by sticking with one or two colors or kinds of

Design by Rydhima Brar of R/terior Studio; photo by Mike Carrero.

Design and photo by Natasha Habermann.

Design by Zandra Zuraw; photo by Erin Little.

material for your pots. This lets the plants do the heavy lifting in terms of decor, while the pots are tying it all together. This is especially true if you keep several pots close to one another, as I do in the bay window of my kitchen. I've chosen to use only terra-cotta and white pottery for my plants. Because my kitchen window is the best window in the house, I've got a lot going on here and I don't want the pots to compete for focus. But if your favorite color is blue, maybe consider using all blue pots, or whatever your heart desires.

Depending on the look you're going for and the amount of space you have, the shape of the pot also comes into play. You can put a skinny straight-up plant (like a snake plant) in either a round-shaped pot or a thin, tall pot. Here, I've put my snake plant in a round basket because I like the contrast between the straight, smooth leaves and the curved, woven container. It would have a completely different feel if I put the same plant in a tall, rectangular pot made of smooth porcelain or cement. Both work. They're just different. I strongly advise you to take your plant with you to the garden store to pick out pots, or bring your empty pots with you to the garden store to pick out plants. It might feel a little silly at first, but trust me, you won't be the first person they've seen do this. And it'll save you the headache of returning things.

Designs this page by Zandra Zuraw; photos by Erin Little.

Once you've got your plants potted and in the right light, there's one last thing to consider, and that's how they relate to other things in the room. If you're grouping your plants together, you want them at different heights. You may have noticed that I use cake stands for this purpose in my kitchen window. In my living room, I have a stand from IKEA and a vintage stand as well. If you see a vintage plant stand (usually metal but sometimes marble, if you're lucky), and it doesn't cost too much, snap it up. They went out of style decades ago but they're really useful. First, they keep a plant from taking up valuable surface space on your tables or buffets. Second, they're portable so you can tuck one in anywhere without having to rely on another piece of furniture for display. And of course, they're meant to prop up a plant so it gives you the height that an empty corner in your living room might need or allows you to get the plant closer to a window.

In terms of mixing different types of plants together, there's really no way to go wrong. Choose plants whose foliage you love. Most areas in your home will look good with a mix of different plant and leaf shapes. If you like a symmetrical look but don't want to use two of the same plant, consider the shape, size, and visual weight of each plant and make sure those characteristics match. The beauty of having houseplants is that they change over time, continuing to help your space evolve.

HANDMADE

We inherently value handmade items

You may be noticing that many of the Slow Styled Home design elements are intertwined, and none more so than handmade items. Several of the elements we've discussed also fall under this "handmade" category. Antiques simply because they were made in a time before mass production. Art is inherently handmade (although this is debatable as we move into the age of AI-generated art). Nature sometimes overlaps with handmade, as you can see in this sculptural rack of hooks in my den, made by a friend from found pieces of driftwood. And as you'll read in the next chapter, Heritage and Culture, I encourage you to seek out handmade items as mementos when traveling to other countries.

Earlier in the book, I discussed handmade elements in bigger investment pieces. This chapter is going to focus on the reasons that incorporating smaller handmade things—either bought or that we made—elevates the experience we have inside our home.

Opposite: A collection of stoneware and ironware artfully arranged. Design and photo by Sean Scherer.

Above: Design and photo by Katie Saro.

WHY BUY HANDMADE?

First and foremost, I believe that the imprint of a human hand left on something hand-made imbues energy that a mass-produced item cannot. When you run your hand over something handmade, you're touching the same object that another human has molded, carved, embellished, twisted, dyed, and so on . . . and that provides meaning. Just as we feel connected to something larger when we stand in awe of a night sky filled with stars and marvel at the scale of the universe, we also can feel a profound connection to humanity and our collective creativity when we hold something made by hand.

In this room by Sean Scherer, you see a wide range of handmade pieces, all working beautifully together because of how they contrast with each other in terms of style and point of origin. What Sean calls the "Flintstone Table and Bench" is a good example of vernacular design. It's utilitarian but still has an elegance about it. It was made by some-one using whatever they had on hand, influenced (consciously or not) by Twig style or possibly Adirondack style, popular in the area in which it was found. Behind that you see a handmade "hired man's bed," a kind of cot used for workers on estates to rest during a long workday. This piece is lighter and more graceful. There's also a handmade cabinet for holding mail and keys from a Catskills hotel. You simply wouldn't be able to repro-duce the amount of soul you feel here if all these things were mass-produced replicas.

I'm not saying everything you own should be made by hand, and I'm not against technology or even mass production in some cases. So what are the objects I'm talking about when I urge you to consider buying the handmade version of something? Let's start with the "extra" things or decorative items in your home. Things you don't neces-sarily need but would like to have. In some cases, we may want multiples of something we already own. Think of a vase or throw or serving dish. I can't imagine any situation where you would *have* to buy a mass-produced vase rather than one that's been hand-made. When was the last time you had a *vase emergency* that required you to drop everything and run to the nearest store that was still open at 9 p.m.? Being more mind-ful when purchasing these extras is an easy way to start the shift from mass-produced to handmade.

The mindset I'm laying out here is especially relevant to people who've been accu-mulating things for a while, don't really need anything new, and have already run through the impulse-purchase-then-donate-to-charity cycle several times. Making a commit-ment to buy handmade when it comes to adding more layers to your home is a way of slowing down and saving money by buying less. Then when you do buy something, you are really supporting a community of makers rather than an anonymous chain store behemoth. When you buy handmade, you're getting both the sensory and emotional experience of connecting to another human, and the quality of something that won't look like it belongs in the trash can a few months after you've bought it.

Design and photo by Sean Scherer.

THE DIY EXPERIENCE

I promise I'm not expecting you to become the next star of a home renovation or living-off-the-land HGTV show. I know DIY isn't for everyone. If you appreciate high-quality, handmade craftsmanship and would rather buy things from artisans and makers, that's awesome! Owning these kinds of objects will add to the decorative and emotional layers that I've been talking about throughout this book. But if you have even a *tiny* inkling to do something in your home with your own two hands, I think you'll get a lot from the experience. The following are some foundational projects.

Walls

I'm sure you've heard this before: the cheapest, fastest way to make over a room is with paint. If you need a hit of dopamine, there really isn't a simpler way to feel satisfied than to paint your room a completely different color. Get the angled brushes to cut in or use painter's tape so you don't have to worry about your edges. After you've done this a few times, maybe you're ready to level it up with a splatter treatment. Katie Saro, one of the most fearless decorators I know, chose to cover her dining room floor with paint splatter and drippings based not on Jackson Pollock (as you might assume), but in reference to a popular device used in old New England beach homes where they'd do this to hide sand that was tracked in on people's shoes. As if this wasn't brave enough, Katie continued the idea onto the bench. The framed artwork is also handmade. It's a huipil garment from Guatemala. The marble table she bought for a song at a thrift store.

The room has the feel of a funky, gotta-be-in-the-know coffee shop that functions as an art gallery and sponsors open mic nights. Yes, it's a bold commitment in terms of claiming a design direction and that may not be for you. But think about how any kind of truly immersive design choice would affect you if you lived with it for a while. Imagine having your coffee here in the mornings and your dinner parties at night, full of candlelight. I think the atmosphere would rub off on you. It would subconsciously nudge your thinking toward new ways of seeing your day-to-day life.

Design and photo by Katie Saro.

Also consider what you can hang on your walls. Here you see a piece of driftwood and an old wooden shelf. A friend of ours found both washed up on the beach, attached them together, and added hooks. We loved the feel of the whole composition but didn't really need it for hanging coats. Instead, we put it on a wall in the den and used it to prop us some photos while hanging pots for air plants and a string of large beads.

Photo by Erin Little.

Here's another example of a big payoff from using paint in a playful way. Katie did a free-form mural in this entryway. She painted the chair an almost neon yellow, taking it from bulky, country quirk to something that looks like it came out of an '80s music video. Katie also happened to replace a set of metal stairs with a wooden spiral staircase to open up the room. I'm not suggesting you have to go that far if you're new to the DIY game and don't have the expertise of a seasoned builder. I'm saying, just think what you can do with a simple can of paint!

The thing about doing DIY projects is that they require you to invest yourself in your home. Not just physically, but in terms of your vision, your dreams, your imagination.

Pillows

Another great project for those interested in dipping their toes into DIY is to make your own throw pillows. I have a sewing machine that I know how to thread and I can sew a straight line. That's pretty much the upper level of my expertise in the sewing department. And I haven't needed to go much further than that to do several projects for my home. Pillows are a simple way to start. You can make an "envelope" pillow without even having to learn to sew in a zipper. You just over-lap pieces of fabric on the backside that allows you to insert a pillow form. And if you really want to lessen the work involved, pillows can be made from napkins and placemats where you've already got most of the edges hemmed.

The fun part in all of this is choosing the fabric. My favorite places to look for options are antique fairs. There are usually a few booths that carry vintage fabric exclusively, and because it's their specialty, it's often organized for easy rummaging. For the throw pillow on this kitchen chair, I found a piece of 1960s bark cloth; for the pillows on my couch, I found some West African, indigo-dyed scraps of fabric that had an unfinished fringe on one end. Rather than cutting it off, I incorpo-rated it into the front of the pillow simply by planning out how I'd cut the fabric into separate pieces. I've made roughly half of all the throw pillows in my home. It definitely saves money, especially when I think about how many pillows I have (I rotate them out frequently, so I have lots in storage, too). But the happiness I feel when I look at them doesn't just come from being thrifty. It comes from knowing I followed my curiosity about pattern and motif, from the freedom to choose fabrics not seen everywhere else, and from the satis-faction of making something with my hands.

Design by Zandra Zuraw; photo by Erin Little.

Design by Aldous
Bertram; photo by
Blake Shorter.

Curtains

With a sewing machine, you can also start making your own curtains, which is extremely helpful on your wallet. For curtains, I often buy the material at fabric stores rather than antique fairs because I need to make sure there's enough yardage available. As with pillows, we're talking straight lines and hemming. Not very difficult, and with the obvious advantage of a custom look. For smaller windows, I've been known to simply use dish-cloths for café curtains. The only thing you need to do there is sew a pocket for the rod. Aldous Bertram has used the idea of valances and curtains in an outdoor setting. It gives him privacy on the patio in a delightful way, adding color and pattern.

Dining Room or Occasional Chairs

Another easy fabric project, one that doesn't even require a sewing machine, is to recover dining room chair seats. Flip the chair over, unscrew the seat and you'll see that the fabric is wrapped around a cushion or piece of foam, and stapled on. Take it all apart, wrap your new fabric on, and staple. I'll do this every ten years or so with my dining room chairs when they need a little facelift.

From there, you might find yourself motivated to move onto reupholstering something. You'll notice I'm not giving step-by-step instructions for this. I think it would be foolish of me to offer a tutorial when it's much more practical to look up a how-to video on YouTube, especially when those videos are made by people who are much more skilled than I. And if I'm only proficient at sewing straight lines, I'm an outright beginner when it comes to upholstery. Not that that's stopped me from trying.

I'm blessed with a nonperfectionist attitude when it comes to DIY, which means I don't get stifled by fear of making mistakes. Granted, my projects might not pass muster if you were paying me to do this. But I'd rather have the fun of trying than be closed off to that opportunity by being overly self-conscious. The bench seat in our living room is a fine example of my not-very-high-standards. Looks pretty good from this vantage point, but if you got up close, you'd see the errors. But, it allowed me to practice a new sewing skill: adding cording around the perimeter of a cushion. Plus,

Above: Photo by Erin Little. Opposite: Design and photo by Sean Scherer.

I bought this fabric in a small, independent shop on a trip to visit my in-laws in Pittsburgh, so it's special for that reason, too.

If you want to see a much better example of skill, here's a sofa Sean Scherer reupholstered for his home. He chose a pedestrian ticking stripe fabric for the Victorian camelback, and I love the contrast. It allows you to use an elegant antique in a more casual setting. The pillow was handmade by his partner, Gary Graham, who is a fashion designer. A sewing pattern for a sleeve is appliqued on top. You just can't get this kind of personalization without going the handmade route.

Lampshades

Another manageable DIY project is to change up a lampshade. I've made several over the years, some with paper and some simply by covering an existing shade with new fabric, using a spray adhesive. In this photo by Katie Saro, she's added upholstery trim around the top of a capiz shell chandelier. And for Natasha Habermann's dining area, she got her parents involved, creating something wholly unique out of scratch. Her dad built the wooden structure, and her mom wove the rope into something that's reminiscent of a lobster trap.

Above: Dining room design and photo by Natasha Habermann.

Opposite: Design by Katie Saro; photo by Kelly Christine Sutton.

CREATIVE THINKING

There are several things I love about making something yourself. You get something custom fit in the exact color, material, or pattern that you're looking for. It's often cheaper—although be careful if this is your only goal: add up the cost of materials before deciding. And it's great if you've got an idea that you want to try out. The following are some examples of ways designers have added a creative spin on a handmade project.

In Natasha Habermann's daughter's room, she installed this lovely wallpaper by Barneby Gates, which happens to be hand drawn. But what I want you to notice are the tiles on the fireplace surround. They were left over from her kitchen redo (a creative idea in and of itself), but what's really sweet are the baby animals hand-painted in blue by her mom, mimicking Delft tilework from the Netherlands.

This guest room, also by Natasha Habermann, had a problematic leak in the ceiling. To fix it, she exposed the rafters, then decided to keep the ceiling open and paint everything white. She wanted the William Morris wallpaper to stop at the place where the original ceiling ended, but also didn't want that delineation to be abrupt. In a genius move, she simply added a copper-colored velvet ribbon around the seam, using upholstery tacks to finish it off.

Design by and photo Natasha Habermann.

Design by and photo Natasha Habermann.

Do you have a home with formal architectural details that you'd like to make a bit more playful? This is what Aldous Bertram has done by adding a quirky green outline to some of his. And if you don't have architectural details, you could paint some in! Or add cutout wooden shapes to cabinets to give a boring '80s kitchen a dose of personality like Katie Saro did here.

Living room design by Aldous Bertram; photo by Blake Shorter.

Kitchen design by Katie Saro; photo by Kelly Christine Sutton.

Living room design by Aldous Bertram, photo by Blake Shorter.

Another thing Aldous has done in several of his homes is create his own draping around beds to elevate an empty bit of space into something romantic and luxurious.

I've never wanted carpet on my staircases out of pure laziness. The idea of hauling a vacuum cleaner up and down the stairs to clean them is beyond my level of interest in home care. But I do love having a pattern on the stairs, which has prompted me to paint faux runners a few times. Currently, I've done a free-hand quasi-cheetah print; before that, it was a wide strip of blue with two stripes toward the outside edges. It looked like a simple, modern carpet. When I repainted

the walls of the entryway a slightly different blue, they competed with the "runner." Even if it was a completely different color, it would have still felt like color blocking, which I didn't love. I realized the missing element was pattern. I do love a good animal print, and I figured organically shaped spots wouldn't be too difficult. I was right.

I'm a middle-of-the-road DIYer. I've had some success with painting furniture, stenciling walls, and découpage. But I've had my share of fails, too. (Needlepoint, knitting, and basket weaving come to mind.) My reasons for starting a project are either because I want something in particular and can't find it elsewhere, or I simply feel like doing something with my hands. Sometimes it's because I'm trying to save money and so I do the parts I can do on my own. Sometimes I'm not in the mood to take on the hassle that inevitably comes with making something myself. And other times, I'm motivated by the pure pleasure of seeing an idea I have in my head come to life. If you really don't want to take on any DIY projects, that's totally fine. But I hope I've at least inspired you to be on the lookout for things made by other people that you can bring into your home. The difference is felt in the touch.

Design by Zandra Zuraw; photo by Erin Little.

HERITAGE AND CULTURE

Where we come from is a creative springboard for where we're going

Why is it we crave individuality, the instinct to differentiate ourselves from others? The desire to be seen as a singular human who leaves at least a small mark on the world? I know there are entire schools of thought addressing this question, led by philosophers and cultural anthropologists who've dedicated their lives to figuring it out, and I'm not one of them. But I'll throw in my two cents and say that I think it's connected to our search for both meaning and purpose. I read somewhere once (probably in a book by one of those philosophers or anthropologists) that "meaning" is what we look for when we want to understand what happened in the past. And "purpose" is what we look for when we want to know what to do in the future. In this book, I want to demonstrate how design elements can represent what is meaningful (such as ancestry and experiences) or what gives purpose (such as family, community, and the planet) to your life.

Opposite: Anne Hulcher Tollett had clients who were moving from London to Richmond, Virginia. That amazing "London Bridge" sign you see in this room actually was found in Richmond—the clients took it as a good omen for their relocation.

Photo by Helen Norman.

BRINGING IN FAMILY STORIES

When I was a sophomore in college, I was lucky enough to snag a coveted "single" in on-campus apartment housing. I had my own bedroom, without a roommate. My first instinct was to claim who I was at that time by adorning the walls with things that no one else would have. I rummaged through my mom's old photo albums and found a handful of black-and-white photos of relatives long gone. They were all studio portraits, capturing the faces and hairstyles, collars and lapels.

In this book, two of the designers featured are very much connected to homes that have been in their families for generations. A few years ago, Katie Saro moved from Dallas back to Minnesota when she was able to buy her grandfather's home, which she's currently remaking as her own. The artwork is by her cousin, Charlie Sesson, that he did when he was in art school. He stood on a thirty-foot ladder with a pen attached to a pendulum and let it swing. Katie says it's about letting go of control, a lesson we all grapple with at some point during our lives. Just like all her previous homes, this one is filled with Persian rugs because her husband, who's Armenian, has always had these kinds of rugs in his life and wants them going forward.

I tell people who are worried about the fragility of old rugs not to sweat it. These rugs have already withstood a great deal of wear and tear and will last at least another fifty or a hundred years. This is far longer than a mass-produced rug bought a few months ago. I've gotten all my vintage rugs from antique shops and fairs, but you can also buy them online. My favorite online sellers are Revival Rugs, de Maroc, and the Vintage Rug Shop. You can find them in the Resources section.

In case you're curious about the term "oriental," it's now considered antiquated and offensive because it comes from a Western perspective that ignorantly lumped all peoples together who Europeans "oriented" as living east of themselves. That's a pretty broad brushstroke! When it comes specifically to rugs, however, the term "Oriental" is still used. I prefer, when possible, to name the country or tribe from which a rug originated. It's just more interesting to know that background than to say a rug is "Oriental." But if you don't know the origin, and you're referring to a rug that is hand-knotted or woven on a hand loom, and made of wool with motifs associated with Indo-Islamic patterns, you're talking about an Oriental rug. If it was made in Iran, those rugs are specified as Persian rugs.

Opposite: Design and photo by Katie Saro.

Design by and photo Natasha Habermann.

Natasha Habermann moved upstate from New York City to be near her parents, who still live in the home her mom grew up in and where Natasha was also raised. In her guest room, she hung two pieces of art illustrating a fox hunt that came from her grandparents when they lived in that home. I love that she's hung these paintings over a wallpaper pattern that's modeled after fishing nets. She and her family spent a lot of time on the coast when she was growing up and the combination of land-based and water-based memories is so personal.

Design by Anne Hulcher Tollett of Hanover Avenue; photo by Helen Norman.

This collection of white pitchers and containers was hiding away in a cabinet. Anne Hulcher Tollett's client had received some of them from her mother but wasn't sure what to do with them. Anne brought them out and used them almost like an art installation in this dining room. The objects become interesting when grouped together because the white-on-white palette brings out the silhouettes of each object.

Kitchen design and photo by Erica Swagler.

Sometimes we honor the heritage of the house itself. Erica Swagler certainly does this throughout her home, balancing the modern-day needs of her family while still respecting the time period during which her home was built. She happens to love antiques, so her home is dotted with them. But even if you favor contemporary furniture, there are still ways to acknowledge your home's history. Anne Hulcher Tollett took an old black-and-white photo of her client's house, had it enlarged, printed on metal, and hung over the fireplace of their 1916 home. (The bunny, by the way, is an antique from a children's playground.)

Design by Anne Hulcher Tollett of Hanover Avenue; photo by Helen Norman.

Photo by Erin Little.

Out of the pieces of our culture, heritage, and family stories, we add meaning to who we are and how we came to be. Even if we don't know all the details of our personal histories, there's a strong pull to imagine who our ancestors were and wonder at the possibility that some of their essence has been passed down to us. That's why seeking out objects that represent where we've come from make such an impact in the decoration of our homes.

In my house today, bits of my family history are scattered about. You wouldn't necessarily know there's a family connection unless I told you. But that's the beauty of being invited into someone's home . . . there are conversational clues out in the open that can deepen your connections to others if you simply ask. I have several tin boxes and wooden crates bearing the labels of my great grandfather's biscuit company throughout the house. Some of them have been passed down to me and others I've bought at antique stores. My friends will text me if they see one and ask if I want them to pick it up because they know about my connection to them.

Designs this page by Zandra Zuraw; photos by Erin Little.

My interest in this part of my family history prompted the creation of our coffee table. I saw an old bakery display table at an antiques store. Painted across the side was National Biscuit Company (yep, that's Nabisco), which eventually bought my great-grandfather's Huston Biscuit Company. The display table was counter height and might have worked as a kitchen island, but not in our kitchen. My husband and I figured out he could cut down the legs to make it coffee table height. Some people may balk at altering an antique in this way. But it wasn't precious or valuable, and I'd rather see something old that's been altered and used rather than see it thrown away. It was simply interesting to someone like me who had a reason to feel a connection. And it's much better than the generic coffee table we were using before.

On that same side of the family, I inherited (aka took from my dad's attic when he wasn't looking) a collection of hand-tied fishing lures. They had been made and framed by a friend of my grandfather's and I remember seeing them in his bedroom when I was growing up. It's a lovely piece in its own right—senti-mental, and the lures themselves are quite interesting. But they also relate to another design element in this book: Nature. As I mentioned in that chapter, I've wanted to live near water for as long as I can remember.

I grew up on the west coast of Florida and spent my summers on a rocky Maine beach and could stare for hours at the waves crashing up around me. Those framed lures may be for lake and stream fishing, but their connection to water is right at home on our staircase gallery wall made up of paintings and objects about the ocean.

Sometimes things you inherit inspire you to rearrange parts of your home. When my mother-in-law asked if I wanted the silver tea service that had belonged to her mother, I was delighted. I wasn't sure if I'd really use it all that much, but I knew I'd regret letting it go. I tried displaying it on two different surfaces in our dining room, neither of which worked. The tea set either looked like it was waiting to be put away somewhere else, or it looked like it was unintentionally left amongst a bunch of other things like clutter. I even tried putting it in our den but that also felt totally out of place. Finally, I realized there was no other solution but to take out a chair and two bookcases from a corner in the dining room and find an antique hutch with glass doors that would house my new prized possession. What got me equally excited about this prospect was that I had, over the years, been collecting interesting antique serving pieces; those could also now have a home outside my closed cabinet doors. And so the hunt began. It's a bit like the book *If You Give a Mouse a Cookie*, and the mouse needs some milk to go with the cookie, then he needs a straw to drink the milk, and so on. I always loved that mouse. One of my tenets in Slow Style living is to actually *use* precious dinner and serving ware. In addition to my mother-in-law's silver service, I'm looking forward to inheriting my grandmother's china from my mom's side of the family. I might "need" an additional piece of furniture for that, too.

Once you start thinking about what connects you to your family history or the culture in which your family has developed, you have a wealth of inspiration to draw from. Was your grandmother a fabulous seamstress? You could collect vintage sewing patterns and apply them like wallpaper to a powder room. Was your uncle an engineer for one of the powerful Detroit motor companies? Maybe you take some of his old tools and use them as a lamp base. If your family tree has a tangled mix of cultural heritage, you can always pull on strands that appeal to you for no other reason than you like how something looks. Do a little DNA research and find your roots. Celebrate your lineage with the crafts and artistry from that culture, create a vignette using history books, hang a tapestry, or make pillows out of fabric woven in that country.

The ideas are endless.

Opposite: Design by Zandra Zuraw; photo by Erin Little.

Portugal is high up on my list of places I want to visit. We came across this large, heavy display case from a Portuguese-American club listing honor roll students in their community. Sometimes it's fun to pick up a piece representing a place you're dreaming of going, even if you haven't been there yet. The little beaded pigeon ornament hanging from the knob I bought on our last trip to Italy from the Guggenheim in Venice. You may know St. Mark's Square is famous for its pigeons, birds that many people find dirty and annoying. But a beaded pigeon? I couldn't resist.

Photo by Erin Little.

A NOTE ON DIFFICULT FAMILIES

Let's be honest. No one has a picture-perfect family devoid of arguments or rifts. Some of us have even suffered abuse within our families. If you don't associate happy memories with your heirlooms, I can understand you not wanting to display them and you may feel this chapter on bringing in your heritage and personal history doesn't apply to you. Of course, you are the only one who can (and should) make that decision and it's more than okay to let these things go if that helps. But let me suggest that, sometimes, bringing some of these objects into your rooms and taking the time to play around with how you'll use them might be a way to deal with past injuries head-on. It may be a way for you to take back control and reimagine your future.

WHAT WE FIND ON OUR TRAVELS

There's always been a market for souvenirs. From Marco Polo and the spice trade, to transporting tulips in and out of the Netherlands, people have wanted to bring back parts of their travel experiences into their homes. For a while, tchotchkes were big business: pennants, shot glasses, postcards, keychains. They fell to the depths of tackiness and then some made a comeback, sought out for their vintage charm. But there's so much more to bring home than the stuff you can grab at the airport.

Presumably you have a reason for spending the time and money to go somewhere. Maybe it's a sporting event and you're looking forward to being part of the fan-frenzied crowds. Maybe it's a hike in picturesque mountains you've seen in photos that's on your bucket list. Whatever it is, if you're intentional about bringing your travels into your home, pay attention to the sense of place you're experiencing. Notice what's standing out to you. What feels different from being at home? Zero in on the colors, patterns, fabrics, natural materials, sounds, smells, and what's happening with the natural light. Journal about it, sketch it out, take photos. Let these be the guide for what you choose to buy.

Cambodia is known for several types of crafts, including lacquerware. Before we arrived, I had sought out a guide who was tapped into the arts and crafts scene in Siem Reap. She arranged a private tour of a workshop where their mango trees provided the raw materials for wooden sculptures and their lacquer trees provided the shiny, viscous liquid used to paint and seal the objects. We chose a fish, one common to the Mekong River. Each white speck you see is a broken piece of eggshell, hand placed by an artisan.

Photo by Erin Little.

The first thing I do when I'm about to travel is learn as much about the culture of that place that I can. It might mean reading a novel or watching a movie set in the city I'm visiting. It might mean learning a bit of the language and getting at least a bullet-point version of the history. Because I'm looking for inspiration for my home when I travel, it always means figuring out the must-have food that's particular to the region, and what kinds of arts and crafts are indicative of the culture. That's where I'll find the treasures I'll be bringing home.

Sean Leffers might think of himself as a traveler as much as a designer. You can see throughout his work how much his experiences in cultures not his own have influenced his design choices. In this room (page 170), he mixes together iconography and objects from Buddhism, Chinese mythology, nineteenth-century Swedish design, and American portraiture. The Buddha is from the ancient Gandhara region (modern-day India and Pakistan) made during the time when Greco-Roman aesthetic ideals were moving east and Buddhism was moving north and west. In it you can see the confluence of two cultures: a distinctly Roman nose with a Gupta brow. The Swedish desk he got on

Design by Sean Leffers; photo courtesy Elizabeth Carababas.

1stDibs.com from a family who had everything made on-site for their farmhouse, specific to its rooms. The statue is of the Chinese Goddess of Mercy and the physical embodiment of infinite compassion (named Guanyin), and dates back 800 years. She represents the fragility of compassion, and for Sean, it's a reminder of how we must care for that fragility. The portraits hit closer to home. They were painted by T. C. Steele, a leader of the Hoosier Group of painters in Indiana, where Sean is from. In the latter part of the 1800s, Steele wanted to deepen his study of painting by moving to Munich. To pay for the trip and his time in Europe, several wealthy landowners of large farms each paid one hundred dollars toward his excursion in exchange for promised family portraits upon his return. These are two of those debts. Sean calls Steele "the original crowdsourced artist."

I believe that curiosity—cultivating it, lavishing attention upon it—is what keeps our day-to-day lives interesting. And I don't just use "interesting" as a throwaway word. When that key ingredient of life is missing, it can make you unhappy or depressed. So if you do have the ability to follow your curiosity, I suggest making that a priority on your busy calendar of responsibilities. In some ways, it's the ultimate expression of self-care. Respectful curiosity in your travels allows you to connect with others in a profound way. In the bedroom, Sean has a large painting by the Argentinian artist Santiago Quesnel on the wall to the left. Sean helped found and is on the board of the Institute for Contemporary Art in San Diego. One of his favorite projects was creating an exhibit of Quesnel's work. On the bed is a nineteenth-century American quilt; the other fabrics are from parts of West Africa where indigo dyeing is revered.

Design and photo by Sean Leffers.

WHAT TO BUY ON YOUR TRAVELS

One question I get all the time is how to incorporate your travel souvenirs into what you already have at home. If you go to China and fall in love with brightly colored paper lanterns, will they look out of place in your Minnesota dining room? The answer is: it depends. (Frustrating, I know.)

To more fully answer this question, I say that if you've decorated according to rigid style categories, then no, a souvenir not in that style probably won't work. By rigid style categories, I mean decorating using things only associated with one "look," such as "farmhouse," or "boho," or "preppy." Obviously, you like things outside of those definitions (maybe those Chinese paper lanterns), so I would ask you, why would you limit yourself to this kind of decorating in the first place? When you throw out the style categories and use the Slow Style approach for deciding how to decorate, it's going to be a lot easier to bring home things you haven't seen elsewhere, things that are unexpected and work next to what you already own. That's where the real magic of a Slow Styled home starts to reveal itself. If you truly don't want your home to look like anyone else's, and you want it to reflect very particular parts of yourself, parts that are wholly unique to who you are, travel is a great source of inspiration.

The truth is that a travel souvenir isn't guaranteed to work with what you already have every time. Sometimes it really will stick out like a sore thumb, but there are ways to reduce the chances of that happening. When you're debating about buying something, take a moment to think about how, where, and when you'll use it. Really picture the room in which it'll be displayed or stored. Think about what you already have in that room. Ask yourself these questions:

- Can you picture this new thing in the mix?

- If not, could you rearrange things?

- Is there something else you have in a different room you could bring in to make it feel more at home?

- Would it make an interesting juxtaposition in color or material with what you already have?

- Would the cultural heritage or the era in which it was made make a compelling contrast, tension, or "conversation" with other things you own?

- If you're buying an artisan-made object, does it come in a range of colors or patterns? If so, could you choose one that would combine nicely with other, similar objects in your home?

Notice I'm not saying the travel souvenir has to "match" anything. I'm just suggesting you should take some time to picture it in your home and trust your gut about whether or not it'll be fantastic or look out of place.

I mentioned earlier that my husband and I almost always look for a piece of art when we travel. If we love the natural landscape, we might look for a painting that captures it. But it doesn't necessarily have to be an obvious representation of the place itself. Sometimes it's the experience of visiting a gallery, meeting an artist, or touring a workshop that draws us in, regardless of the subject matter. Then, we're bringing something into our home that we love for its own sake and that has the added benefit of reminding us what we were experiencing on a particular trip.

We have a window seat in our living room where I regularly change up the pillows. The two on either end that you see here are from a restaurant in Ho Chi Minh City (formerly called Saigon in southern Vietnam) called "Propaganda," a tongue-in-cheek reference to communism. The illustrations on the pillows are of "proletariat" workers (farmers, fishermen, and so on), which also covered the two-story walls of the restaurant creating a bright, lively atmosphere for the best noodle dish I've ever eaten. Even though I didn't already own anything with this childlike playful style, I knew the colors in the pillows would fit in with the colors of other pillows I already own.

Design by Zandra Zuraw; photo by Erin Little.

In this photo, you see a mix of things I've picked up on our travels. Vintage Zane Grey novels that I've been collecting for years make a great backdrop to whatever other things I layer in front. I bought my first one at a used bookstore during our first trip to Santa Fe, New Mexico. I liked the Wild West subject matter for a souvenir, plus the fact that the author's first name began with a "Z" made it an appealing choice. Two more treasures from Cambodia are on the buffet: a beautiful Buddha sculpture I found at a gallery inside Raffles Hotel in Phnom Penh, and the table runner, which is actually a modern scarf. The pattern on the scarf is modeled after the checkered design co-opted by the Khmer Rouge militia and then reclaimed by contemporary citizens as a symbol of holding onto their heritage while moving beyond the horrors of war. To the side of these treasures—and not pictured in the photo—is a vintage wine bottle from Portugal to remind me of my wish to visit there and a handwoven basket from

a trip to Charleston, South Carolina, where I watched generations of women making intricate designs from native sweet grass.

The basket is from the American South, the bottle is from Portugal, and the scarf is from Cambodia. Here's why this collection feels cohesive: They are all *woven* elements, tying together a visual foundation for the rest of the vignette. The fish, which you saw in a previous photo, is shiny, sleek, and rather modern looking, which is a nice juxtaposition of materiality against the faded desert colors of the books, whose tattered, jacketless covers are made of worn linen. Furthermore, the fish stands out because it has a horizontal orientation against the vertical pattern created by a row of books. It doesn't look like I bought everything at the same time from the same place. But it doesn't look disjointed either. Paying attention to color, shape, pattern, and materials ensures you develop a cohesive feeling.

ON THE SUBJECT OF CULTURAL APPROPRIATION

When you travel, I'm suggesting you collect and then display objects from histories and cultures that are not your own. I want to recognize though, that there has been a lot of discussion around the problem of cultural appropriation, which references a power imbalance between those who have taken artifacts or imagery from others, without permission or without even an understanding of the meaning behind them. Sometimes it's fairly clear that something has been stolen or reproduced with complete ignorance of the history of the object, not to mention indifference toward any harm toward the culture that may be associated with it. But sometimes, frankly, it's hard to know when that line has been crossed because there are no mutually agreed upon definitions of the line itself.

Design by Zandra Zuraw; photo by Erin Little.

Is it okay for me to hang wooden masks that I'm told my grandfather bought on a trip to Haiti years ago? Is that different from me buying a piece of art created with traditional techniques from the artisans themselves on a trip to Cambodia? I'd like to think that when we educate ourselves on where these pieces come from, how they're made, and the meanings behind them, we are celebrating a culture that's not our own, rather than appropriating it. But there will be some people who feel differently, and I can see their side of things, too. My own guidelines include buying objects made by the people who know something about them through their own lived experiences, paying a fair price for these objects, and educating myself on the craftsmanship that goes into making them.

Sean Leffers sums this up so well for me. His own personal belief system is in the power and beauty of universal humanity. He's bought many things from people who ethically source and sell antiques and handmade objects. For him, "Meeting dealers while traveling is one of the best resources for the transfer of knowledge over time." He places a lot of value on the people who collect these stories of material culture, and they're the next best thing to meeting and buying from the artisans, artists, and craftsmen themselves. As he so beautifully puts it, "When you hold material culture in your hands, you're holding the unbroken bonds of humanity over time."

Acknowledgments

Sarah Woodward, Beth and Chris Bean, Nikky McCay, and Dallas Roberts—you've been around for this whole design-fueled life I've been trying to create and have always made me feel it was possible. I thank you to the moon and back.

Shout out to the High 8 and its 2 honorary members . . . my life wouldn't be the same without you. And thank you to my whole family, especially my mom, who's been my forever-fan and there for it all.

I truly wouldn't be writing this book if it weren't for my agents Alan Nevins and Jacklyn Saferstein-Hansen of Renaissance Management. Your wisdom and clear guidance have been invaluable. Thank you to my editor, Jennifer Adams, for your careful consideration of every word and photo, along with the entire team at Gibbs Smith. You all have given me multiple injections of confidence, which has been more important than you probably know. And a special thank you to Madge Baird for taking a chance on this project in the first place.

Austin Mill, you are the perfect person to launch this book, and I thank my lucky stars that we met long before I even knew I wanted to write a book. This whole endeavor required the friendship, trust, and enthusiasm of all the designers featured, and I'm so honored to have collaborated with you. Your talent continues to inspire me.

Quinn, you remind me every day of what's most important in life. Calvin, I can't even begin to express how happy it makes me to come to you for design advice. I'm so proud of you. And my deepest love and gratitude to Pete for, well, everything all the time. You know it and I know it. I couldn't have done this without you.

Resources

These are a few of my favorite people, places, and things. Many of the people here I've interviewed on the Slow Style Home *podcast.*

ACCESSORIES

Reflektion DesignFor goods sourced from Ghana, Kenya, and Ugandareflektiondesign.com

Noma Collective
For goods sourced from around the world
nomacollective.com

Stocker Studio
For laquerware made in Cambodia (such as Zandra's fish sculpture)
stocker-studio.com

ANTIQUES

Kabinett & Kammer (owned by Sean Scherer)
kabinettandkammer.com

Sean Leffers Antique Textiles
seanleffers.com/textiles

Ariene Bethea: Dressing Rooms Interiors
dressingroomsinteriorsstudio.com

Melissa Parks (AKA Megillicutti): Warehouse 55
warehouse55aurora.com/collections/megillicutti

Debbie Mathews Antiques
debbiemathews.com

The David Alan Collection
thedavidalancollection.com

The Crompton Collective
cromptoncollective.com

Toma Clark Haines (AKA The Antiques Diva)
For personalized buying tours in Europe
antiquesdiva.com

ART

Ron Johnson
His artwork is shown in multiple galleries.

Sarah Boyts Yoder
sarahboytsyoder.com/home.html

Angela Chrusciaki Blehm
angelachrusciakiblehm.com

Grace Keogh
oldnewhouse.com/collections/contemporary-wall-art

John McCaw
Abend Gallery
abendgallery.com/artist/john-mccaw

Eikoh Hosoe
en.wikipedia.org/wiki/Eikoh_Hosoe

Santiago Quesnel
lacaprojects.com/artists/santiago-quesnel

Sabra Field
www.sabrafield.com

Treacy Ziegler
treacyzieglerfineart.com

Miguel Lopez Mora
instagram.com/miguel_lopez_mora/?hl=en

Ruth Scotch
ruthscotch.com

Amy Donaldson
Gallery: Gaia Contemporary
amydonaldson.com

Sandra Pratt
Gallery: Giacobbe-Fritz Fine Art
sandrapratt.com

William Crosby
portlandartgallery.com/artist/
william-crosby

Barbara Bowles
barbarabowles.com

DECLUTTERING

Peter Walsh
peterwalshdesign.com

Monica Leed
simplyspaced.com

Tracy McCubbin
dclutterfly.com

DESIGNERS

Aldous Bertram
aldousbertram.com

Angela Chrusciaki Blehm
angelachrusciakiblehm.com

Anne Tollett, Principal Designer
and Owner, Hanover Avenue
hanoveravenue.com

Beth Diana Smith
bethdianasmith.com

Carmen Rene, Principal Designer
and Owner, Aquilo Interiors
aquilointeriors.com

Erica Swagler
instagram.com/living_in_a_landmark

Katie Saro
katiesarostudio.com

Natasha Habermann
natashahabermann.com

Nicole Cole, Founder and CEO/
Principal Designer, Vestige Home
vestige-home.com

Rydhima Brar, Founder, R/terior
Studio
rteriorstudio.com

Sean Leffers
seanleffers.com

Sean Scherer
kabinettandkammer.com

Trevor Fulmer
trevorfulmerdesign.com

Zandra Zuraw
slowstylehome.com

FURNITURE

Roger + Chris
sofas, chairs, ottomans
rogerandchris.com

GALLERIES

Abend Gallery
Denver, Colorado
abendgallery.com

Gaia Contemporary
Santa Fe, New Mexico
gaiacontemporary.com

Giacobbe-Fritz Fine Art
Santa Fe, New Mexico
giacobbefritz.com

Liz Lidgett
Des Moines, Iowa
lizlidgett.com

UGallery
Online only
ugallery.com

Portland Art Gallery
Portland, Maine
portlandartgallery.com

Shiprock
Santa Fe, New Mexico
shiprocksantafe.com

HOTELS

*Places I've Stayed with Fabulous
Interior Design*

Hotel Clermont
Atlanta, Georgia
hotelclermont.com

33 Main
The Berkshires, Massachusetts
thirtythreemain.com

Cornell Inn
The Berkshires, Massachusetts
cornellbb.com

Ace Hotel & Swim Club
Palm Springs, California
acehotel.com/palm-springs

Woodhouse Lodge
New York State
thewoodhouselodge.com

The Parador
Santa Fe, New Mexico
paradorsantafe.com

The Wayfinder
Newport, Rhode Island
wayfindernewport.com

Greydon House
Nantucket, Massachusetts
greydonhouse.com

Touraine
Philadelphia
touraineapts.com/p/the-suites

The Vintage Round Top
Round Top, Texas
thevintageroundtop.com

LIGHTING

Ted Bradley
tedbradleystudio.com

PAINT

Clare
www.clare.com

RUGS

Landry & Arcari
Rugs, designed by Trevor Fulmer
and others
landryandarcari.com

VINTAGE RUGS

Revival Rugs
revivalrugs.com

The Vintage Rug Shop
thevintagerugshop.com

de Maroc
demarochome.com

WALLPAPER AND MURALS

Fine & Dandy Co.
fineanddandycompany.com

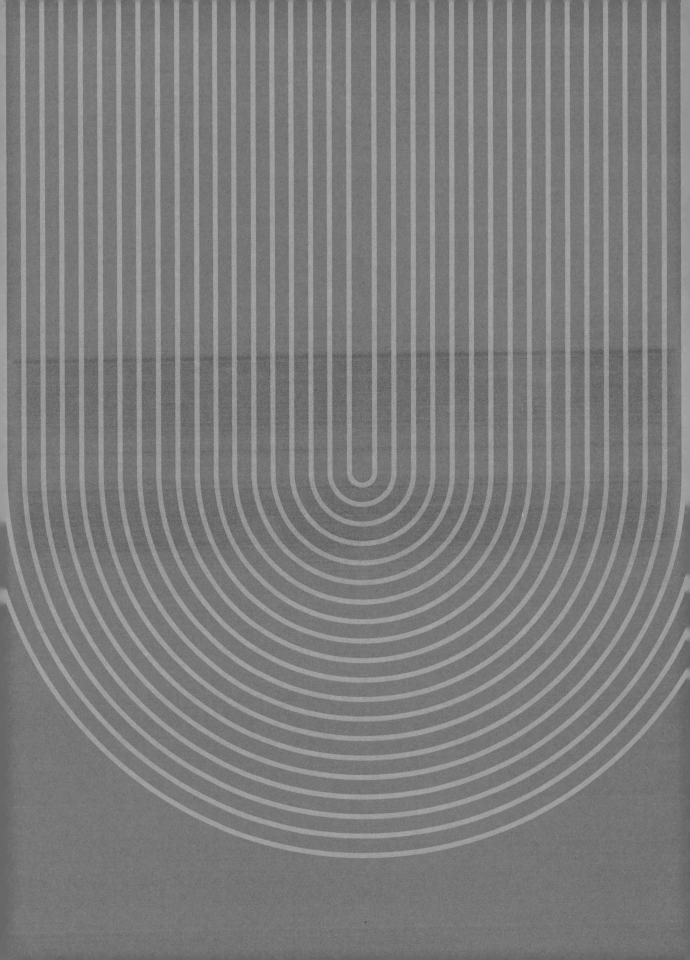